OPERA WONYOSI

OPERA WONYOSI

Wole Soyinka

INDIANA UNIVERSITY PRESS
Bloomington

First Midland Book Edition 1981

Typeset in Great Britain
Printed in the United States of America

Library of Congress Cataloging in Publication Data

Soyinka, Wole.
  Opera wonyosi.
  I. Title.
PR9387.9.S606 1980 822 80-8384
ISBN 0-253-13435-8
ISBN 0-253-20259-0 (pbk.)

Foreword

Since *Opera Wonyosi* was written and performed (December 1977), the African continent has been rid of the two singularly repellent and vicious dictators who feature in the play: 'President-for-Life' Idi Amin and 'Emperor-for-Life' Jean-Bedel Bokassa. A third, no less odious and bloodthirsty, 'President-for-Keeps' Macias Nguema of Equatorial Guinea has not only been removed from power; he came to a well-deserved end on a hangman's rope. 1979 proved a very bad year for the continent's spawn of political and moral mutants, and a warning for those who have managed to survive that unprecedented Year of the Purge.

But how did (and do) they succeed in retaining power so long?

Primarily by the active connivance and mutual protection games of other equally guilty (or nearly so) incumbents of seats of power on the continent. In some cases there was genuine ignorance, carefully nurtured by the falsified reports of their national diplomatic representatives in the various countries, expatriate élites motivated by personal self-interest. Assiduously courted by agents of repressive power in such countries as Uganda, flattered, pampered, privileged and sealed with their own acquiescence from the realities of the nation upon whose miseries they feasted, these panders fed their governments with glowing reports of the monsters to whom they were assigned, and dismissed the outcries of the peoples as Western-orchestrated noises designed to discredit the true heroes of African nationalism.

I recall, with shame and disgust, the bland dismissals of a highly placed official of the OAU, whom I encountered in Addis Ababa early in 1977. To every demand that he, and others like him, accept the duty to make known to his masters and his people the truth of the Ugandan situation, he had only one reply: Idi Amin was a genial, witty and unpretentious African whose generosity could not be faulted. He had just returned from a three-day visit to Uganda, at Amin's own invitation where, he insisted, he was literally given the freedom of the country. Beyond this personal, *privileged* experience, his horizons did not extend. Let us take note of the existence of these moulders of 'informed' public opinion.

Let us take note also of another type, whose sophistry so readily overwhelms, deadens or excuses all obligation towards even a vocal commitment to the victims of such inhuman malformations. For such 'dispassionate' observers of society, the Bokassas, Nguemas of this world do not exist except as the products of specific socio-economic causes. This malformation of the critical intellect of African neo-Marxists will require fuller attention in its proper place; for now it is only necessary to affirm that a distinction is recognized between the mouthers and opportunists on the one hand; and the genuine but theoretically obsessed on the other. The medium of such literary genre as *Opera Wonyosi* will be reserved for the former while we will attempt to 'dialogue' with the latter in brief and at length whenever occasion demands it. At the foundation of our rejoinders will be found an uncompromising concern for the social values of literature, a recognition of the limitations and its potential, and an assertion of the writer's rôle as being merely complementary to that of the politician, sociologist, technocrat, worker, ideologue, priest, student, teacher etc., not one which can usurp one or all of these roles in entirety without forfeiting its own claim to a distinctive vocation.

A quite favourable review in the University of Ifé based journal *Positive Review* nevertheless laments the lack of a 'solid class perspective' in *Opera Wonyosi*. Translated in practical, drama-turgical terms, the reviewer desires an adaptation which would latch a class exegesis on to my parade of clowns, fools, villains, mass-murderers etc. in their arbitrary setting of a Nigerian ex-patriate colony in the (then) Central African Empire. Let us make it wearisomely clear that the province of the artist, while it does not exclude a direct interest in the class, socio-economic, psychological, and other possible promoters of his characters' being, on stage or on paper, is not such as cannot validly manifest itself in any given work without taking into its immediate provenance all or more of these various contributors to the *history* of that character, or his fate at curtain-time.

A play, a novel, a poem, a painting or any other creative com-position is *not a thesis on the ultimate condition of man*. Even Marxism recognizes that revolutionary theory is incomplete in itself; the praxis, the operation of that theory when power is seized by a revolutionary party that professes the theory is what constitutes the infallible test of that theory. *Opera Wonyosi* is an exposition of levels of power in practice—by a satirist's pen. To ask for a 'solid class perspective' in such a work curtails creative and critical options and tries to dodge labour which properly belongs to the socio-political analyst. The Nigerian society which is *portrayed*, without one redeeming feature, is that oil-boom society of the seventies which every child knows only too well. The crimes committed by a power-drunk soldiery against a cowed and defenceless people, resulting in a further mutual, brutalization down the scale of power — these are the hard realities that hit every man, woman and child, *irrespective of class* as they stepped out into the street for work. school or other acts daily amnesia.

Indeed, I am definitely in agreement: 'Art can and should reflect, with the "dominant" temper of the age, those vital, positive points which, even in the darkest times, are never totally absent.' Equally is it necessary that art should expose, reflect, indeed magnify the decadent, rotted underbelly of a society that has lost its direction jettisoned all sense of values and is careering down a precipice as fast as the latest artificial boom can take it. Was, or was this not a period of public executions which provided outing occasions for families, complete with cool drinks, ice-cream, akara, sandwiches and other picnickers' delights? We must demand if the class and socio-economic analysts of society found, or indeed attempted to find a way to end this coarsening assault on the sensibilities of the populace, and most unforgivably, the development of children? Or was it perhaps dialectically correct? A nauseating spectacle that could, by a suitable election of historical conditions, be programmed into the *scientific* surrender of our 'irrational' impulses that simply insist through the medium of art: a child should not be manipulated into a tacit acceptance of the public slaughter of his kind.

What does the class conflict have to say — or even more relevantly, what did the class conflict have to say about the epidemic of ritual murder for the magical attainment of wealth? Of those syndicates which kidnapped and murdered victims *of all classes* in order to convert their vital organs to wealth talismans? We know of course that this latent ailment developed into an outright epidemic in the wake of the oil boom and Udoji Wages Commission increments — that is obvious. The course is easily traced. What the writer will not accept is the irrational claim that a work of social criticism must submerge its expression of moral disgust for the anodyne of 'correct' class analysis. At the very least, the former takes the subject away from the escapist rhetoric, from conveniently remote and 'scientific' causes and rubs the faces of the collaborators — the audience — in social shame, in the sewer of their material existence. We do not intend to give any 'intellectual' audience the comfort of seeing their material situation as the *inevitable* consequence of their socio-historical condition. We pronounce: 'Guilty' on all counts, then we leave the rest to the potential re-shaping force of society — among which we, the writers, consider ourselves — to work upon.

The dangers posed to society by those who, on the one hand, paint a bleak, unrelieving picture of an amoral, uncaring society and on the other, the ideologues who batten on the supposed 'class-perspective' short-comings of the former but cannot evolve an effective idiom for their own active social alternatives would, I am certain, constitute a relevant comparative study for yet another class of neo-praxists. Those of us who see no reason to present a utopian counter to the preponderant obscenities that daily assail our lives and, whose temporary relief is often one of 'sick humour', will continue to press this line of confrontation by accurate and negative reflection, in the confidence that sooner or later, society will recognize itself in the projection and, with or without the benefit of 'scientific' explications, be moved to act in its own overall self-interest. Any serious student of the sociology of theatre who witnessed *Opera Wonyosi*, and the reactions of audiences would not dare deny the social impact of that experience on a truly wide spectrum of the audience, across all class divisions — from the 'lace' madams to Oduduwa Hall kitchen-hands; from the Military Governor to the victim (or victim acquaintance) of his soldiers' code of anti-civilian conduct; from the university don to the parks attendant. . . . theatre is rooted in the responses of such audiences for whom it is meant, not in the theoretic speculations of even genuinely committed ideologues. To suggest that the turning up of the maggot-infested underside of the compost heap is not a prerequisite of the land's transformation is the ultimate in dogmatic mind-closure. All evidence in the material world of theatre and society asserts the opposite.

'WOLE SOYINKA
ILE-IFE
MARCH 1980

OPERA WONYOSI was first performed on the occasion of the University of Ife Convocation, 16 December 1977 in the University main theatre, Oduduwa Hall. The Cast, with the University of Ife Theatre, and Students was as follows:

DEE-JAY	Hamed Yerimah
ANIKURA	Gbemi Sodipe
AHMED	Akin Akinyanju
DE MADAM	Bola Popoola
CAPT MACHEATH	Segun Bankole
MATAR	Sola Soile
POLLY	Gaynor Bassey
HOOKFINGER JAKE	Peace Wakama
DAN DARE	Kola Oyewo
BABA	Laide Adewale
JIMMY/LOOKOUT/VENDOR/VERY RICH GENTLEMAN	Uko Atai
JERUBABEL	Yomi Fawole
INSPECTOR BROWN	Dolu Segun
EMPEROR BOKY	Gbola Sokoya
AIDE/PATIENT	Kola Oyewo
SUKIE	Shade Agbaje
JENNY/NURSE	Yemi Adebayo
OLD SUGAR	Gboyega Ajayi
LUCY/NEIGHBOUR	Buchi Chukwuogor
COLONEL MOSES	Femi Euba
PROFESSOR BAMGBAPO	Kole Omotoso
DOGO/ALATAKO/OFFICER	Ayo Lijadu

PRIEST, BEGGARS, GANGSTERS, LAYABOUTS, WHORES, GOON-SQUAD:

Caroline Agbowoerin, Mosun Falode, Florence Oni, Olu Okekanye, Muyiwa Dipeolu, Peter Fatomilola, Ola Awofade, Andrew Akaenzua, Stella Obioha, Oyilade Igbekele, Tunji Ojeyemi and the Company.

The Orchestra, under the direction of Tunji Vidal:

CLARINET	Karen Barber
	Felix Olaniyonu
VIOLIN	Ajibola Mesida
DRUMS	Muraina Oyelami
	Thomas Adefisan
TUBA	Frank Olude
PIANO	Tunji Vidal

Scene I

(*The Orchestra plays 'Mack the Knife' in the background.*)

DEE-JAY I'll just introduce myself. I'm your M.C.D.J.—Master of Ceremonies Disc-Jockey. Or Master of Ceremonies or Disc Jockey. Or simply Dee-jay. Take your Choice. I'm hosting this show. One time we called it the Way-Out Opera—for short, Opera Wayo. Call it the Beggars' Opera if you insist—that's what the whole nation is doing—begging for a slice of the action.

And don't think it's the kind of begging you're used to. Here the beggars say 'Give me a slice of the action, or— (*demonstrating*)—give me a slice off your throat. Man, some beggars! You know what, why don't you just make up your own title as we go along because, I tell you brother, I'm yet to decide whether such a way-out opera should be named after the Beggars, the Army, the Bandits, the Police, the Cash-madams, the Students, the Trade-unionists, the Alhajis and Alhajas, the Aladura, the Academicas, the Holy Radicals, Holy Patriachs and Unholy Heresiarchs—I mean man, in this way-out country everyone acts way out. Including the traffic. Maybe we should call it, the Trafficking Opera. Which just complicates things with trafficking in foreign exchange. Nice topical touch. Man, this country whips you right out on cloud Nine! I'd better bring you back to earth with a song about that universal species of humanity—and if you haven't heard Louis Armstrong do his own thing with good old Mack, man, just where you been? One—a-Two—a-Three—take it from there Baby. Let's go.

(*The Company stroll in, in character, and in their various groups—Beggars, Goon-Squad, Mackie's gang etc— promenade about the stage while they sing the song* Mack the Knife.)

Now the shark has teeth like razors
And he shows them in a fight

[1]

All Mackie has is a flick-knife
And he keeps it out of sight

Where the night flows dark and silent
There you'll find men lying dead
Was it plague that really killed them
Or a fee to Mackie paid?

You'll recall that Lagos doctor
In Ikoyi slashed to death
The report lies in a Closed File
Mackie vanished like a wraith

Was Mackie seen in Badagry
Where another seemed to drown?
Did our expert of convenience
Fix the man who won't pipe down?

Would you like a marble headstone
And be martyred in a cause?
Go and meddle in Igbeti[2]
And a slab for free is yours

For it takes more than the darkness
To protect one beast of prey
When there's interest joined to interest
All we can do is pray.

DEE-JAY   Now you know where we're at. If you're still uncertain, let me tell you that your Deejay isn't feeling all that cocksure himself. But there is to be a Coronation. An imperial coronation, first in Africa — at least in the last few decades or so. Emperor Boky, Boky the Cocky, no less — and if you think that's mere boasting, ask him how many daughters presented their credentials when he advertised for his long-lost daughter from Indochina. He confirmed the claims of one and married the others. Man, he's wa-a-a-ay — Out. Also known as Folksy Boksy on account of he likes to meet with the folks. You dig? The common folks, like vagrants, felons and — dig this — school children. Actually rubs feet with them — well, on them sort of — he's gone beyond shaking hands — wow, he's ahead man! But so am I on the

[2]

story. And this is your M.C. Dee-jay turning the scene to introduce to you Chief Anikura King of Beggars. A professional artist who belongs to the School known all through the ages as Con Art. In short, a master of the psychology of charity.

(Anikura emerges. Kicks awake the bundles of rags and cloth which have been strewn all over the floor. Human forms emerge, slink off, taking their rags with them.)

Anikura's Song

> Christians smooth and sleek, wake up
> Moslems in gold turbans, fake up
> Now tell me you pieties
> Is there one jot, bar niceties
> To choose from your cozening make-up?
>
> You bankrupt your neighbour every day
> And smother good consciences with pay
> Then on Sundays and Fridays
> You deny all your fun-days
> And the next week resume your dirty play.
>
> Pray do not change your Con technique
> For to many, life isn't a picnic
> And outside the church
> Or the mosque is a wretch
> Who depends on your mood philantropic.
>
> But look out, one day you will find
> That pus-covered mask hides a mind
> And then — boom! — oga sah [3]
> What's that blur? — oga sa?
> With a red flame fanning his behind.

ANIKURA What a cushy job Moses had — what with God on his side and all. Simply hit his staff on a rock and all that water came gushing out. I have to do what I can without that kind of help. And getting money out of people is rather like that magic of Moses. Well, those who have no powers of miracle must make do with psychology. I understand human nature. Maybe Moses understood God but I doubt

[3]

it just the same. I also understand my society—which is more than could be said for him. He was always getting caught out, surprised. Me, no. That's where science triumphs over magic. The only problem I have is novelty—something new to clutch the heart-strings and loosen the purse-strings. Every model is soon *deja vu*. But I forget, you don't speak French do you? I'm a first-generation Nigerian exile here. Came here during that Civil War we had over there. This used to be Central African Republic—still is, but I hear it's going to become something grander very soon. So what with one thing and another, I parlay vous fransay. But we try to keep us the old home culture around here, so not to worry, I know you're going to feel at home. You know what they say of us Nigerians don't you? We know how to take care of business. We are always getting thrown out of one country or another but, while we last, well—we do know how to take care of business. So, with your permission, I beg leave to make hay while the sun shines through the imperial arse-hole.

(Knock on the door.) Enter.

AHMED   Ranka dede.[4] You are Chief Anikura.

ANIKURA   I am thus addressed.

AHMED   You own the business 'Home from Home for the Homeless'?

ANIKURA   Indeed.

AHMED   I was recommended to you.

ANIKURA   *(takes out a notebook, puts on his glasses.)*
Name?

AHMED   Chief Anikura, I am totally destitute, my parents' house was burnt over our head during the Civil War. My father lost his life and my mother is still missing . . .

ANIKURA   *(writing furiously)* It's a good story. A variation on the old line. They've heard too many tales of that problem here. I may as well tell you that every other Nigerian who comes here is a victim of the war. Still, there was that little extra touch you added—mother still missing. Oh there are lots of missing mothers but you see, you could add that you came looking for her here and got stranded. You were duped. Defrauded. Gave your money to a fellow Nigerian to change and he disappeared. Yes, they'll believe you. They know that any Nigerian will rob his starving grandmother and push her in the swamp. You'll do.

[4]

AHMED   Oh no Chief. I would hate to libel my fellow countrymen.

ANIKURA   If only you knew how much your countrymen libel their mothers! But you take that story and stick to it. Memorize it, avoid unnecessary embellishments and you are well away.

AHMED   Perhaps you're right. I was telling it straight only yesterday, on the corner of Avenue Charles de Gaulle and the Place de la Republique . . .

ANIKURA   *(rising in a fury)* Place de la Republique? Oh, so you were the scab. Poacher. Trespasser. Illegal entrant. Were you well flogged?

AHMED   I don't understand it Chief. Two gentlemen suddenly appeared and set on me. They flogged me nearly senseless, then gave me your card.

ANIKURA   You were lucky. Or maybe they had just lunched. *(Turns to a map on the wall.)* Take a good look at that. This shaded area is entirely within my jurisdiction. We call it New Ikoyi.[5] There we try to retain all the living styles we had at home, down to the naming of the streets. The rest of Bangui is shared with the foreigners — the natives that is — a rather unsophisticated lot if I may say so. We had to help them with certain details of organization, so in effect, we have a *laissez passer* — passport to you — to work in their own territory. You want to work across the border or in New Ikoyi?

AHMED   I think I prefer to feel at home. I'm not likely to get lost there.

ANIKURA   Don't be so stupid. Our sector is marked by sign-posts of up to ten feet of garbage, so you can't miss your way. Now choose your sector within our national boundaries divided into 19 districts. Which do you prefer? Different rates of course. Central areas more expensive than the suburbs . . .

AHMED   Chief. I think I must let you know that I have only . . .

ANIKURA   The prices are listed on the board. And considering the fact that I've provided you with a story . . .

AHMED   But I came with my real story.

ANIKURA   Useless. I wouldn't even sell you a Union card with that tale. It's the variation I added which turned it viable. A thousand CFA. Three Naira if you like. We accept our national currency here. And so — *(makes a rude noise)* — to that Foreign Exchange Decree you've just passed.

[5]

AHMED   Please Chief Anikura, One Naira.

ANIKURA   Two. And only because of the beating you had yesterday. Our job is to induce Charity in others, not practise it ourselves.

AHMED   One Naira fifty please Chief Anikura. It's all I have. *(Holds it out.)*

ANIKURA   Plus 50 per cent of your weekly takings. Don't think you are not constantly watched. Some of your donors may be among my Auditors. It is strictly forbidden to keep a closed bowl or use your pockets. You will be issued standard bowls — different shapes but with identical mechanism. You deposit the money, press a button and the false bottom opens and the coins fall in. It opens only one way. Don't try to tamper with it.

AHMED   As if I would dream of such a thing.

ANIKURA   You will. But don't try to make your dreams come true. Or you'll find yourself doing the Cripple — and that won't be make-up either. Name.

AHMED   Ahmed, Chief.

ANIKURA   *(Looks him up and down.)* Hm. You'll need a costume all right. That brings it to 70 per cent of takings.
(Begins to inspect costumes)

AHMED   Chief . . .!

ANIKURA   Oh you do the strangled-voice anguish all right. *(mimics)* Chief. *(laughs)* Just remember it doesn't move me. Give and it shall be given unto you. *I* know my Bible. Do you?

AHMED   Actually I am a Moslem.

ANIKURA   Oh? Of course with a name like that you would be. That makes you something of an interesting proposition. We don't get too many of you coming to me. There's a marabout among the natives who takes care of people like you. We expatriates are mostly Christians if you get what I mean. We practise Charity Begins at Home. Your faith isn't against that is it?

AHMED   Oh, not in the least.

ANIKURA   I'll tell you why I don't seem to mind you at all. Indeed, if for once I may be emotional, why I seem even to heartily welcome your presence in our establishment. *(raising his voice)* My dear . . .

DE MADAM   *(from inside)* Are you calling me Chief dear?

ANIKURA   Tell me, our fellow the Life President, what's he these days?

[6]

DE MADAM I think he's back to the Christian fold.

ANIKURA Are you sure?

DE MADAM *(emerging)* Well, he returned from Libya a fortnight ago didn't he?

ANIKURA But that's when he became converted.

DE MADAM That was the first trip when Ghadafi promised him 20 million dollars. He got converted on the spot. Then he went back last week to ask for contribution for his coming coronation and the Arab man told him to go home. So he changed back to christianity.

ANIKURA *(to Ahmed)* You see, the power of money. Oh, may I present—my consort and right-hand man-and-woman rolled in one—Madam Cecilia Anikura, better known in these parts as—De Madam.

AHMED Your servant ma'am.

DE MADAM Delighted I'm sure.

ANIKURA He is a Moslem he says. Not a bad thing to have on our books if the Life President Emperor-to-be should change back to Islam again. Fashions change with the leader you know. In the two weeks Emperor Boky was a Moslem you had more civil servants and professors coming in and out of mosques than there was population in the country. Not to talk of businessmen. Everyday the personal column of the papers, you know, the Change of Name Section . . . I, formerly known as Fidelis Desiree Michel Charlemagne now wish to be known as Mohammed Idris Suleiman etc. etc. *(He seems to find a satisfactory one among the costumes. Changes his mind. Looks him up and down.)* Can't really find one to go with our story. Mind you, you're starting at the right time, being on the eve of coronation and all. (Hauls them all up.) Look, you pick one. My consort will adjust as necessary.

AHMED *(recoiling)* What's that?

ANIKURA *(in formal lecturing voice)* These represent the five types of misery most likely to touch people's hearts. The sight of them brings about that unnatural state of mind in which people are actually willing to give money away. *(Selects one.)* That's the cheerful cripple—victim of modern road traffic. We call it the Nigerian special. The next model— War Casualty. Can't stop twitching you see. Now that first puts off the public. But the sight of the war medals he's wearing softens them. The third model—we call it the

Taphy-Psychotic.[6] It's got a whip you see. He rushes around in a frenzy as if he's going to flog you. But that's where we put in the variation. He doesn't actually flog you. He stops with his hands raised and breaks into an idiot's grin—and you realize he's only soft in the head. You are so relieved you give him money. Number Four. Victim of Modern Industry. Collapsed chest. That sits down well with the business tycoons. Remember the Cement Bonanza? Well, to clear those ports they had the hungry sods moving the cement bags round the clock. Pay was— good to decent, and every labourer earned all the overtime he could. What no one bothered to tell them was the effect of breathing in cement dust 12 to 18 hours a day. It's called Fibrositosis. Same as in asbestos factories. Wait, I'll tell you all about it in a song. (*Looking up at Dee-jay.*) Accompaniment please.

DEE-JAY Ladies and Gentlemen, Chief Anikura and present Company will now sing a song entitled: Big Man Chop Cement; Cement Chop Small Man.

Big Man Chop Cement; Cement Chop Small Man

A labourer's life is a healthy one
It's fresh air from dawn till the sun goes down
Clean exercise; see how those muscles bulge
Power beyond you my bookish don
And what if a man does himself indulge
At night when the bloody labour is done
Every cloud has its silver lining
Clouds of cement ensure my dining
A mound of eba washed down in palm wine
And overtime pay brings the suzies in line.

Chorus:

I know now it's true—life is a wheeze
The proof's in my lungs when I sneeze
Well, my chest is congested
But the port's decongested
While I breathe like a dying accordion
Seven more years says the surgeon
And you end on a slab of cement
It ends on a slab of cement.

[8]

No thought for tomorrow, this Jack's all right
Grind all day long and grind all night
Udoji[8] will come when things grow dull
Then watch me jump on a Saturday night
I tell you this cat's right on the ball
Like a sailor in town, high as a kite
Twelve-inches platform, dig the sky-scraping geezer
Superfly dandy, sharper than razor
Easy come, easy go, God bless Udoji
And the season of ships and cement orgy.

From port to horizon the ships lay spent,
Cement in the holds, on the decks, cement
And I gave up my nights of leisure and fun
For overtime pay makes the worker content
Right round the clock I had a good run
The money came handy, now I repent
A man's lungs for clean air is meant
Not for breathing in clouds of cement
And overtime pay comes to mere chicken feed
When the cement tycoon has filled out his greed.

Chorus.

ANIKURA Well now to the next model. *(Turning round suddenly with the costume before him. Ahmed recoils in horror.)* A blind Man, heart-breaking very effective. *(He notices Ahmed's reaction for the first time. Bawls.)* He feels pity! My God, look at you. He actually feels pity. You feel the same way as the passers-by should feel. You're only fit to be begged from. Lead him away — give him the Bleeding-Heart outfit. And we'll have to change your story. You won't get far with the original one. Your new story is that of the Good Man Ruined by Kindness. Successful man run to seed. Grace to grass. Show him the costume my dear. Follow her and come out for inspection. *(Exit De Madam.)*

AHMED Where do I keep my own things?

ANIKURA *I* keep them. Property of the firm.

AHMED Ah, Allah, these clothes are the very last things belonging to me. They were the last things bought me by my mother before she vanished. *(Anikura fixes him with a long look.)* I'm sorry Chief, I'm very sorry.

[9]

ANIKURA   Be off before I change my mind. And don't forget to leave your shoes.

AHMED   Chief!

ANIKURA   Don't you take off your shoes in the mosque? Allah, what airs! *(Madam Anikura returns with an outfit which she throws at Ahmed, pointing to the changing room.)* Where's our daughter?

DE MADAM   Polly? Upstairs, of course.

ANIKURA   Was that man here? The fellow who always sneaks in when I'm out.

DE MADAM   Don't be so suspicious, Jonathan. There isn't a finer gentleman alive than the Captain. I think he's taken a real fancy to our Polly.

ANIKURA   Hm!

DE MADAM   If my eyes aren't deceiving me, Polly has taken a fancy to him, too. I see a match.

ANIKURA   Use your head, Cecilia. If Polly had a husband he'd soon have us in his grip. No doubt about it. Do you think she can keep her mouth shut in bed any better than you can?

DE MADAM   It's a fine opinion of our daughter you have.

ANIKURA   The worst, the very worst. She's hot for anyone.

DE MADAM   Well, she certainly never got that from you.

ANIKURA   I'm a Master mind, not a Super-stud. And whatever else he is he is first and foremost a gold-digger. It's my money he's after. It can't just be her virtue because I'm sure she disposed of that a long time ago.

DE MADAM   What a thing to say! Jonathan, you're just an ignorant brute.

ANIKURA   Ignorant? Well you tell me this gentleman's name then.

DE MADAM   He was always simply called 'The Captain'.

ANIKURA   You haven't even asked him his name. Did she meet him on a blind date?

DE MADAM   You'd hardly expect us to ask him for his birth certificate — and him kind enough to ask us to a dance at the Octopus Disco.

ANIKURA   Where do you say?

DE MADAM   At the Octopus Disco. We stopped there for a drink.

ANIKURA   At the Octopus Disco? That's where to get picked up all right.

DE MADAM   It's a respectable place! And the gentleman never laid a hand on me or Polly except with his lace gloves on.

ANIKURA   Lace gloves . . .

[10]

DE MADAM Yes, he always wears lace gloves.

ANIKURA And a stick with an ivory handle? And gold chain on patent leather shoes.

DE MADAM *(hopefully)* Real gold?

ANIKURA Pure gold. Smuggled from Lebanon specially for him by his Alhaja, one of many. At least before *their* Civil War. Those Lebanese you know, the Jews of the Arab World. Hm. I still don't understand how everybody is the something of somewhere else, not just something in his own right.

DE MADAM *(thoughtfully)* We have no Middle East contacts you know. And they say there is plenty of lace and gold coming in from there.

ANIKURA What's this now? You want to go into the smuggling business? Don't be so common.
(Ahmed comes out from the Fitting room.)

AHMED Chief Anikura, will you please give me a few hints.

DE MADAM *(sighs)* They all want to know what to do. As if begging isn't an instinct where he comes from.

ANIKURA He's an idiot. *(To Ahmed:)* Come back at six o'clock tonight and you'll be given all you need. Now get out. I want to think. *(He strikes his thinking pose.)*

AHMED Thank you, Chief, thank you so much.
(Exit Ahmed.)

ANIKURA *(Short pause.)* Now I'll tell you who this fine gentleman with the lace gloves is. It's Macheath — Mack the Knife. *(He rushes out and is heard shouting.)* Polly! Polly!

DE MADAM Good God! Mack the Knife! Holy Virgin! Polly! Polly! Oh what has she got herself into! I always said that daughter of mine would come to no good. Polly!
(Anikura comes back.)

ANIKURA Polly hasn't been home. Her bed's not been touched.

DE MADAM She's been out to supper with the lace merchant. I'm sure of it, Jonathan.

ANIKURA I hope to God she is with the lace merchant. I hope she aims no higher than the lace merchant. But will she?

The Song of Ngh-ngh-ngh (Sung by Chief Anikura and De Madam)

DE MADAM Oti o. Ngh-ngh-ngh. [9]
Rather than spend all her nights with her love
She chases class, she chases class

[11]

And who's got the class? Who's got the class?
It's khaki and brass. It's khaki and brass
So rather than spend all the nights with her love
She's planting the seeds of a brass-khaki class
And taking the salute of the Army as they pass.
(Obscene gesture by Anikura on 'Salute')

ANIKURA   Oti o. Ngh-ngh-ngh.
Once his white collar was as high as she gazed
Oh how she adored the ink on his cuff
And how she would swear, how she would swear
Ever to cherish the smooth with the rough
But fashion and time all her oaths have erazed
His clerical sweat is the worst social smear
Which even a Honda makes no easier to bear.

DE MADAM   Oti-o. Ngh-ngh-ngh.
But who will deny that love is no match
For contracts galore, for foreign exchange.
And who's got the clout? Who's got the clout?
Who *can* swear to me, I shall ne'er do without?
The ex-politician who's not worth a scratch?
Or Mr Professor? The Perm-Sec? A Chief?
Well, time anyway has proved each one a thief.

BOTH   Oti o. Ngh-ngh-ngh.
You think I regret love's obvious demise?
Not on your life! Do I look mad?
But why pick a loser? Why pick a loser?
A petty-cash crook? Now isn't that sad?
We know it's the big fish the net's sure to miss
While your small-time bandit earns lead perforations
But come, we must act. Enough perorations.

Scene II

DEE-JAY   Deep in the Bidonville of Bangui known as the Nigerian
Quarter by the natives but christened New Ikoyi by the
Expatriates, the bandit Mack the Knife celebrates his
marriage to Polly, daughter of Chief Jonathan Anikura,
Friend of the Poor, Proprietor of Home from Home for the
Homeless.

[12]

(*Enter MATAR, with torchlight and pistol.*)

MATAR   Hands up, if anyone's in here.

MACK   Well, is anyone here?

MATAR   No, empty. Perfectly safe for a wedding (*pointing his torch everywhere. MACK goes out and returns with POLLY wearing a wedding dress.*)

POLLY   But—it's a stable.

MACK   No, it's the Polo Club.

POLLY   It *is* a stable.

MACK   Don't let's start the day with arguments my dear. A stable is where Jesus Christ was born. I don't aim that high, all I want is a quiet wedding to my own sweetest, dearest Polly. (*kisses her*) I assure you it's the Army Polo Club. We've been loaned their lounge—the horses' lounge of course. I ask for the roomiest.

MATAR   A lot of our people will reckon this a very chancy thing you're doing Mack. Pinching Anikura's only daughter right under his nose.

MACK   Who *is* Anikura?

MATAR   He'll call himself the poorest man in Bangui.

POLLY   But Mack, you can't be thinking of having our wedding here. Polo Club or not, it's nothing but a stable. How could a minister come here? This is supposed to be the happiest day in a girl's life.

MACK   My dear little girl, if Christ could consent to be born in a stable, one of his own Ministers can administer communion in the same place. The furnishings will be here in just a moment or two.

MATAR   Furniture this way!

(*Enter BABA HADJI, DAN DARE and HOOK-FINGER JAKE carrying furniture, crockery etc. The stable is quickly made to look like a loud, over-furnished drawing-room.*)

MACK   Rubbish!

JAKE   Wish you the best of luck. (*Brings in a big painting of the once fashionable Nigerian 'naive' style.*) Now, you'll never guess it, but ten years ago, we'd have called this rubbish. But there were tourists looking for local culture kicks, so . . . there you are. Oh, talking of kicks, the old American collector who owned this thought culture was dearer than survival—we had to put in a few kicks to persuade him otherwise. Nothing serious . . .

MACK   I said No Bloodshed!

[13]

DARE Nor was there. A broken rib or two I think, maybe a case of heart attack — cardiac arrest I think it's called these days — but definitely no blood.

MACK I feel sick when that happens. It's bad business. You'll never make good businessmen. Cannibals maybe, but businessmen, never!

DARE Wish you the best of luck. This quadraphonic set, dear madam, belonged only half-an-hour ago to Mrs Professor of Physiotherapy, University of Bangui. You'll probably hear some complaint from that direction about her person, *(giggles dirtily)*.

MACK Animal! Do you mean you molested her?

DARE I didn't. That's her complaint.

POLLY What's all this furniture?

MACK Do you like it Polly?

POLLY *(crying)* But . . . killing all these poor people, just for a bit of furniture.

MACK And such rubbishy stuff! I *am* ashamed. And you are right to be upset. Quadraphonic set, none phonier. Naive painting — what do you think we are? Collectors? And of course you had to be so cheap as to bring a black-and-white television set? Black and white! Just what throwbacks are you? What age do you think you're living in? Even radio is coloured these days, if you ever listen to the news. I suppose none of you even thought of bringing a table.

BABA A table!

(A big covered object is brought down. Uncovered, it reveals a fully equipped banquet table.)

POLLY Oh Mack, I'm so unhappy. I just hope the minister doesn't come.

MACK My wife is completely upset. How often does it happen I get married? Yet you've got to upset my wife right from the beginning.

JAKE Dearest Polly . . .

MACK *(knocks off his hat)* Dearest Polly! Dearest Polly! I'll shove your head down your guts you cheeky sod! Dearest Polly! Since when did you get so familiar? I suppose you've even slept with her.

POLLY Mackie!

JAKE I swear to you . . .

BABA Madame, if there a few odds and ends you need, we'll go

[14]

out again . . .

POLLY No. Except we have nothing to sit on.

MACK Unscrew the legs off the quadraphonic.

DARE Done. Plus the speakers we have another six seats. Are we expecting a large company?

MACK Christ, look at them! Apart from Baba, none of you even thought of getting properly dressed. After all, this isn't the wedding of a nobody. And Polly, do get busy with that spread of eatables.

POLLY Is it all stolen Mackie?

MACK Polly, you disappoint me. All this stuff has been merely liberated.

POLLY And if the police come in?

MACK That's no problem. I'll take care of it.

BABA Besides, today all the police are lining the streets. The Emperor is making a tour of inspection for his coronation arrangements.

POLLY Fourteen forks but only one knife.

MACK What a mess! That's the trouble with beginners. No style. But you'll manage won't you dearest Polly?

DARE We concentrated on bringing only the classy stuff. Look at the finish on that television set for instance. You don't miss the colour with wood like that.

MATAR Sssh! Permit me Captain . . . *(Opening the magnum of champagne.)*

MACK Come here Polly. *(They pose for congratulations.)*

MATAR Permit me, Captain, on behalf of everyone here, to offer you, on the happiest day of your life, at the zenith of your career, . . . its turning point, as it were . . . to offer you our heartiest congratulations. *(Shakes Mackie's hand.)* Chin up boys!

MACK Thank you. That was very nice of you Matar-boy.

MATAR *(Shakes Polly's hand, pats Mackie on the back.)* And it was spoken from the heart. Well, keep your head up, old chap. I mean—so to speak. And may the old . . . never go *(demonstrating)* limp.
(Roars of laughter from the men. Mackie suddenly grabs Matar's hand and gently forces him to the floor.)

MACK Shut your trap. Keep your smutty jokes for Kitty—she's the right slut for them.

POLLY Mackie, don't be so common.

MATAR You're a fine one to complain. Lucy has told me some of

[15]

the ones you've told her. Mine are lavender water in comparison.

POLLY   Lucy!

(Mackie slowly draws his sword-stick.)

JAKE   This is a wedding Mack.

MACK   A fine wedding, eh Polly? Putting up with all this vermin. You'd never think your friends would let you down like this.

POLLY   *(uncertainly)* I think it's a very nice wedding.

BABA   Of course it is. No one's letting you down. *(To Matar)* Your Kitty is as good as anyone else. There's no finer whore between Bangui and Kano I swear. Come on now with the present my lad.

MATAR   *(A little mollified. Offers Polly the gift.)* Here you are then.

POLLY   Oh, a wedding present. That's very kind of you Mr Matar. Oh look Mack, a night-gown. Isn't it lovely.

MATAR   *(eyeing Mack)* Another dirty joke I suppose?

MACK   It's all right. I don't want to press a point on this happy occasion.

MATAR   Very big of you, Captain.

POLLY   Oh, it is so wonderful. I am so happy. I haven't any words for it. You are all so kind.

DARE   Well wait till you see this *(uncovers a slim futuristic object)*. Latest in grandfather clocks. A genuine Seiko.

POLLY   A Seiko?

DARE   Those Japanese will make anything. This grandfather clock is the first of the kind. No hands. *(Presses a button.)* See? Pure quartz, computerized and fully automatic. Not many countries have any use for it but our people tell me it sells by the hundred at home. Only Nigerians fancy culture you know. This one had been sitting in Monoprix downtown; thought it was time it came where it would be appreciated.

POLLY   But it's so . . . so conspicuous.

DARE   The only one in town, in the Empire in fact. It's a fashion-setter.

POLLY   I mean, it will be easily traced.

DARE   You let the Captain worry about that Ma'am.

POLLY   Ah well. Thank you for taking so much trouble for me.

DARE   No trouble Ma'am.

POLLY   *(tearful)* It's a pity we have no house to put it in.

MACK   Think of it as just the beginning Polly. All beginnings are difficult. Now clear some of the stuff away so we'll have room to eat.

(They start boxing some of the presents.)

MACK This is the best food to be had anywhere today. And that is no idle boast Polly. The best. Shall we start?

BABA Splendid plates. From Hotel Intercontinental. Same firm as makes the Emperor's cutlery.

DARE To tell you the truth ma'am. Everything is the same as the emperor will have on his coronation. The salmon is from Lafayette, by special appointment Fishmongers to His Imperial Majesty. Specially flown from France last night. No problem slipping in among the crates at the Airport. Came through the V.I.P. lounge — a Right Royal Salmon I tell you.

MACK I promised you a royal banquet.

JAKE *Imperial* banquet if you don't mind Captain.

MACK Have some caviar. *(Reads)* 'Guaranteed one-hundred per cent caviar from the Caspian Sea.

BABA That must set back the Treasury a quid or two.

DARE Don't gobble up your eggs like that Jake. The mayonaisse is dripping all over your chin.

JAKE There is nothing wrong with my way of eating eggs.

MACK There is plenty wrong with the table manners of all of you!

BABA Nothing wrong with the food though. A little too rich for my tastes mind you, but then our Captain only gets married once in his life.

(A titter from Matar. He chokes on his food.)

MACK Are you also finding the food too rich Matar-boy?

MATAR Oh no, just something someone said. That was rich all right.

MACK I cannot say I appreciate your sense of humour on an occasion like this.

JAKE I'll bet you've never had truffles like that, Polly. Mack has it everyday. Has it delivered at his mobile address every morning with the newspaper. You've landed all right. I've always said Mack'll make a fine match for a girl with refined feelings. Said so to Lucy yesterday.

POLLY Lucy? Mack, who *is* Lucy?

JAKE *(embarassed)* Lucy? Now you mustn't start getting the wrong ideas about that.

(Dare is making frantic gestures behind Polly to silence Jake.)

POLLY *(seeing him)* Is there something you want Mr Dan Dare?

[17]

Well, what were you going to say Mr Jake.

JAKE Nothing, nothing. If I'm not careful I'll be biting my tongue.

MACK Slicing it off you mean? What have you got on your plate Jake?

JAKE Well, I think . . . yes, I think it's that stuff you called caviar.

MACK I see. And what have you got in your hand?

JAKE My pocket-knife Captain.

MACK I could have sworn it was. And you were going to eat caviar with your knife. And not just a knife but a pocket-knife. Not to mention the fact that it looks rusty from here.

JAKE That isn't rust Captain. It's blood.

MACK Blood. You hear that my dear. He eats caviar with a knife. With a bloodstained knife. Oh Polly, you'll have a heart-breaking job before you can teach these ruffians to act like gentlemen.

BABA By the way whose blood was it?

POLLY O-oh. *(Bursts into tears.)*

MACK Now look what you've done, you silly old man.

BABA I am sorry. I was just wondering if it was anyone we knew.

MACK Shut up! Can't you all understand my wife is very sensitive?

JIMMY *(bursting in)* Captain, I think we've got visitors.

BABA *(looking round the door)* Nonsense, it's the Prophet Jerubabel. *(Enter Jeru pronounced Jèrú)*

MACK *(smoothly)* Good evening Prophet Jeru.

JERU *(looking round)* A stable. I like that touch. Captain Macheath, my dear erring brother, my proverbial lost sheep whom I consider it my duty to return to the fold . . .

BABA I knew he could account for his sponging around.

JERU Let me assure you how much I consider it a veritable act of Divine Providence that he has guided your feet to this significant abode that is — to put it literally — the very cradle of our religion.

JAKE *(offering the plate)* The salmon is good Prophet.

JERU Ah, fish. A veritable sacrament. Was our good lord not himself the Divine Fisherman?

MATAR *(to Dan)* I thought you said the fish came from Paris.

MACK Do make yourself comfortable Prophet Jeru. I am deeply honoured that you took the great trouble of finding your way here.

[18]

POLLY   Oh thank you, thank you Prophet. Now I know that my marriage is truly blessed.

JERU   *(mouthful of fish)* Blessed? I'll say it is. I have here the special bottle of Holy Water which has just come from the Holy City, Jerusalem . . .

BABA   Prophet, a little of this champagne?

JERU   I accept it in the name of the Miracle at Cana. It was a wedding too if I may remind you.

JAKE   I give up.

MACK   You are uneducated Jake. Don't take on better men than yourself.

POLLY   Why not a hymn now please Mack. Now that the Prophet is here, it would make everything so nice if we could have a hymn.

MACK   A hymn it is. A hymn in honour of Prophet Jeru.

DARE   Oh, Captain . . . *(he stops, a little embarrassed.)*

BABA   Go on, don't be so bashful.

MACK   What is it?

DARE   Oh well . . .

JAKE   He has a song. Composed by his very self.

MACK   Well well, in my honour?

DARE   In honour of our good captain and his wife.

POLLY   Oh, they are all so nice to me Mack. Really nice. And you say such rude things about them.

MACK   I *know* them. They have a heart of gold I know, but I can't cut them up just so we can see it more often. All right, let's have the song.

Wedding Song for Polly and Mack
(Sung by the Entire Company)

Hail, pair of turtle-doves
Perfect of earthly loves
All hearts go out to you
Envious of love so true
Live every happily
Raising your family
Both long to cherish
This our very wish.

Daughter of House of Fame
With mind as clear as flame

[19]

No Ph.D. degree
Can match your pedigree
Base be that rank or file
Who thinks to match your style
Dear Belle of our Delight
Belle of true Delight.

To you our Captain brave
Terror of King or knave
Long life, prosperity
Free from asperity
Nay, never shall you bow
Low at the Bar Beach show [10]
Though if that must be so
Bravely, bravely go.

MACK   *(During the singing Mack exhibits signs of torture. Polly is however radiant with delight. Jeru is blandly beaming. On the last lines however, he explodes:)* Less of the graveyard humour if you don't mind.

JIMMY   *(bursts in)* The cops! This time it is the cops! The Commissioner himself.

BABA   Yes, it's Tiger Brown and no mistake. Security Expert from Nigeria on loan to the Emperor since the old civilian days. *(sighs)* Why doesn't he go back home?

MATAR   How could he? Don't you know why he was loaned in the first place? Glad to get rid of him.

JAKE   Add to that, he feels at home from home, among us.

MACK   *(As Brown enters)* Make yourself at home Commissioner.

BROWN   *(offended)* Commissioner!

MACK   All right. Make yourself at home you old scoundrel.

BROWN   Is that the young lady?

MACK   It gives me great pleasure to introduce my old friend and brother, known in popular parlance as Tiger Brown. And this is my own beloved fiancée soon to be my wife, Polly Anikura. *(Brown is startled, stares at Polly.)*
The wedding party is complete at last since we now have what amounts to official sanction . . .

BROWN   Official sanction! Oh Mack, did you have to pick on the Army Polo Club? Breaking and entering, and . . . oh christ, I recognize that salmon.

MACK   Have some, Commissioner.

[20]

BROWN *(accepting it)* I was detailed to protect that right through the V.I.P. lounge. It came from Paris . . .

DARE See?

BROWN How did it get here? Oh my god . . .

MACK Does it taste all right?

BROWN *(unhappily nibbling)* I suppose so . . .

DARE Then there's no harm done, I left enough for the imperial banquet.

MATAR What's going on here anyway? Why is he here? Why is he always snooping? I don't trust him.

MACK *I* do.

MATAR Why doesn't he go back home?

MACK Sit down! Shut up and listen. Polly my dear, I want you to understand tonight, our Wedding Night why you need never worry about Commissioner Inspector Brown, Officer of the Nigeria Police on Loan to the Centrafrique Empire — then Republic — in the bad old days, and stayed on ever since out of deference to the worse new days. You see in his person the individual in whom the present ruler of Centrafrique reposed his trust — his absolute trust in the bad old days, and has learnt to increase that absolute trust in the worse new days. You see before you one in whom the President, then Life President, then Emperor has never ceased to rely and who, despite this precarious honour, has never failed to remain my friend through the various vicissitudes of status that have beset his patron, and consequently, himself. This friendship is mutual. Never, never have I in my humble capacity as safe-breaker and multiple murderer failed to share the proceeds of my adventures with Tiger Brown. And never, never, well, almost never — has he organized a raid without giving me just that little hint in advance. Give and take, give and take is what it takes is how to live. To Tiger Brown!

(Excepting Matar, they all toast: Tiger Brown)

BROWN *(He's been examining the table-cloth)* Unusual in these parts . . .

MACK Persian damask. I had hoped to drape, not just the table but the very walls in that latest Nigerian favourite called Wonyosi. But the ban . . .

BROWN Surely you don't allow trifles like bans to bother you.

MACK It bothers the suppliers from home. The shops here are still waiting for their orders to arrive. We can't rob them of

[21]

what they haven't got can we?

BROWN Mack, the camaraderie! It's what I find so irresistible . . .

MACK You remember those good old days?

BROWN Old Soldiers never die.

MACK You and I together . . .

BROWN What can others understand of this?

MACK Last crumb . . . last drop of blood . . .

BROWN Even if we finally went different ways, but isn't that life?

Khaki is a Man's Best Friend
  (by Mackie and Brown)
  Khaki is a man's best friend
  The girls seem to favour the trend
  So one fine day I upped and enrolled
  With patriots and others, mean and bold
  And I dreamed of the deeds I would do
  And I glowed with the glory of me
  For what is a man but the sum of his power
  To kill or to spare, to make the world cower
  So one fine day, I upped and enrolled
  With patriots and others, mean and bold.

Chorus:
  'Secession' cried one; the other — 'One Nation'
  For oil is sweet, awoof [11] no get bone
  The task was done, the nation is one
  We know who won and who got undone
  No thought of keeping his body one
  It's scattered from Bendel to Bonny Town.

  Now I was one of the frisky trio
  Who staked out the night-spots, *con brio*.
  There was Johnny the Soak, and Pele the Dandy
  Loathe they were to leave their pal Randy
  For they dreamed of the deeds we would do
  And they glowed with the glory of us Three
  And they pictured in 3-D the power of man
  To spare or to kill, to approve or to ban
  So one fine day, they upped and enrolled
  With patriots and others, mean and bold.

  Now Pele, named for his footballing hero

[22]

Found war, as a game, was — Zero.
He was blown up in Uyo, while wine-loving Johnny
Lies drinking his fill of the marsh of Bonny
And I dream of the deeds they could do
And I sigh with the waste of all three.
Randy's the name sir, just the name, only in name
And that, you'll excuse me, is a damn bloody shame
For a man who one fine day upped and enrolled
With patriots and others, mean and bold.

Well, power is power whatever the name
The Khaki sure makes up for the shame
Civilians are sheep, just hear them bleat
When my good Taphy whip clears the street
And to think of the things they could do
Yet they take all this bullying shit from me
Well one can't distinguish in matters of vengeance
Some made the loot while we took the chance
When one fine day we upped and enrolled
With patriots and others, mean and bold.

Scene III

DEE-JAY But you must be dying to know what's going on in the imperial cranies of Emperor Boky, otherwise known as Folksy Boksy. What preparation is he making towards his coronation? Why is it that the Nigerian population in Centrafrique have not been booted out as undesirable aliens? Well, we can't answer that latter question all at once, but we can provide a link in the geographic situations. Hi Boksy, come on out, man. Stepping high if you dig the beat. Yeah — a-one, a-two, a-three, a-four; a-
. . . *(Enter Emperor Boky and squad, in formation. Like a seasoned Sergeant-Major, he brings the squad to a coordinated halt.)*

BOKY Listen you fools. I am a revolutionary. You know the motto of my mother country — *(Lifts hat as he does each time he mentions France or 'mother country')* — France. *Liberte. Egalite. Fraternite.* I am an egalitarian. If I were not an

[23]

egalitarian I would not be among you dregs, you scum, you *residue de bidet*! But I'm an egalitarian. I have the common touch. I am a commoner. But I am·not common. Get that clear. You are clearly common. I am not. Better let that distinction sink into your head and seep always onto your tongue. I don't believe in slips. Slips of the tongue and things like that. It may cost you your tongue or worse.

For instance, Napoleon. Emperor Napoleon was a commoner. He was not even French you know. Just a Corsican. Even at that time they didn't just hand round French citizenship for every pirate or Mafia-type. You had to earn it. So Napoleon was not even a frenchman to begin with. Took him quite some scheming to become one but he finally made it, so there it is.

And he was a revolutionary. You may not remember, but France is the cradle of revolution. Every revolution in the world began in France. And Napoleon it was who eventually placed our mother country on the map. We have to emulate him. Enough.

I have condescended to be with you today not to talk politics but culture. You must know that our mother country, not content with being the cradle of revolution is also the cradle of culture. So understand this — in this empire . . . em, nation, culture is on our priority list.

And that, cretins, is why we are going to participate in Festac Seventy Whenever. To demonstrate our culture. African culture. Revolutionary Culture. Our presentation must be revolutionary. South Africa is in the throes of revolution. Therefore, I shall teach you something of South African culture. It takes the form of a dance to which we can give the appropriate title, 'Putting in the Boot'. Never mind what they call it down there. Now, a revolutionary dance must possess what we Marxists call social reality. So we are going to adapt this dance to the social reality of our progressive Centrafrique Social Experiment. Boots!

AIDE *(rushing in, gives him a pair of Wellington boots. Boky examines the soles)* Fool! Cochon! Serf! Rebel! Where are the hob-nails?

AIDE But these are just for rehearsals your Imperial Majesty.

BOKY *(freezes)* That is not yet official. You are guilty of gross

[24]

indiscretion. You are not to be trusted. Take him away and cut out his tongue.

AIDE *(prostrating)* Comrade Life President!

BOKY Drag him out. Out! Wait. Stop. Cut out his tongue and send that silenced item to my friend Idi Amin, with my compliments. No. Stop. Send Amin the entire wretch and add that his tongue is not to be trusted. He'll know what to do. Take him out. *(Exit Aide screaming, dragged out by Guards.)* Hm. Strictly between you and me, that Amin gives himself airs. Not satisfied with being a windbag he gives himself airs *(pause with deliberate emphasis)*. Not a windbag but gives himself *airs. (He turns slowly to the parade.)* Wind. Airs. *I* think that was witty. *(They roll on the ground laughing. He watches for some time, then turns to the bodyguards)* I want an example. Just one. *(He covers his eyes with one hand and, with the other, blindly gropes for a victim. Two men drag him off, screaming.)* Wit is culture. If you are not cultured you are not French. Tention! At ease! *(He turns back to the audience)* I was saying . . . oh yes, that windbag. But he's also an ape. You know, he apes. He apes me. I appear in a uniform — an official uniform understand — Amin sees me, and straightway he orders a duplicate, complete with medals, plus a few more he's dreamt up. I earned my medals fair and square — in action. Indochina. North Africa. I've travelled and seen action. And then to make it worse he carries his own much better. Got the size for it you know. I didn't like that photo of him and me together. It was as if it was taken on a tossing ship — actually, it was my medals weighing me down on one side, but he didn't feel his own at all. Of course mine are pure gold — trust him to resort to a trick like gold-plated aluminium. No class. Anyway, what does he do, gives himself Victoria Cross, Long Service Medal, Medal from the Crimean War, Order of Florence Nightingale — oh it's really too embarassing. And then he's a pig. Yes, a pig. You know what a pig is don't you? And you know what a pig does with graves. Well, it's on account of Idi Amin — Moslem though he calls himself — that real Moslems don't eat pork.

(Turns slowly to the squad.) They fling themselves down with forced mirth. Enough! Where was I? Yes, I was about to dilate on the tactics of one-upmanship.

[25]

Right. So there was I, constantly embarassed by this apishness. I made myself Life-President, he followed suit. I thought maybe I'd beatify my person and become a Saint. But I knew him. He'd simply add another title to his court list—Field-Marshal and Dr Saint Alhaji Idi Amin, D.S.O., V.C., V.D. . . . oh I mean . . . er . . . V.C. etc. Well, that's how confused the man is—Saint Alhaji. Like wearing Israeli paratroop wings to confer with Arafat on Zionist aggression. Typical Aminian idiocy—oh he makes me blush for poor Africa that pig does.

Oh, does that surprise you? We Frenchmen blush easily you know. It's a sign of French sensitivity. We are emotional, sensitive, much too *raffine* when compared to the English. You should have seen me crying at the graveside of Daddy—you know that great Immortal—General Charles de Gaulle, father of modern France. Yes, I wept buckets. *(Raises his hat for a moment's silence.)* It was the French in me coming out. All emotion you see, we the French. But I was saying—Amin forced on me my coming elevation you know. He'd become a gross caricature of everything I represent, so the only choice left was to aim far above his horizon—nothing less than a black Napoleon. Now you must admit that was original thinking—that was really outclassing that nigger—I mean, how do you top the Imperial crown? No way baby, no way. Enough! I hope you all came with recording machines, because this is the last time you will be privileged to enjoy my condescension. After the imperial crowning, protocol will be so strictly observed that only God will be granted the occasional interview—and even then, strictly by appointment. *(Examines his watch.)* Time for Culture. I know I should sing for you, but you can't do much with the voice in the way of Social Reality. With boots on the other hand, with or without hob-nails . . . Ready!

Rhythm Section! Ready . . . Two—Go! One-Two-Three-a-Four! One-Two-Three-a'Four! Come on! One-Two-Three-a'Four! One-Two-Three-a'Four! One-Two-Three-Dig! In! One-Two-Three-Heels In! I said Stomp! Stomp! See their eyes—Dig In! Skulls! Imperial Stomp! Stomp! Stomp! Studs In! Studs In! Toe-caps! Grind! Grind! Crotch movement! Crotch! Dig In! Dig In! Spinal Column! Aim for the Pelvic Junction! Pelvic Junction!

Grind! Grind you bastards, I said Grind! Where's the expert from Nigeria? Inspector Brown! There you are — take over while I put some Life into them.

BROWN   Certainly your Imperial Majesty, but er . . . could I quickly make a report sir? A slight unrest in the city . . .

BOKY   Unrest Inspector Brown? Did I hear unrest?

BROWN   Hardly even that your Highness . . . just a minor disturbance, and already contained.

BOKY   No unrest or — disturbance — is to be considered minor on the eve of my coronation Inspector Brown.

BROWN   Your Imperial Majesty may himself condescend to consider it minor sir, when I inform him that the disturbance involved only minors. Schoolchildren to be precise, your Highness.

BOKY   Schoolchildren? Mes petits enfants?

BROWN   Nothing but the usual high spirits your Excellency. We were able to gather that it had something to do with their new school uniforms.

BOKY   School uniforms? And what, Inspector Brown, did school uniforms have to do with schoolchildren? These — pupils were required to wear them, nothing more.

BROWN   Well er . . . your Imperial Highness is er . . . as our Intelligence reports have already suggested to your Majesty . . . er . . . there has been a degree of disquiet over the er . . . I mean since the . . . er your Imperial Highness's decree on the uniforms. A demonstration took place — only school pupils involved Your Highness. They have all been locked up for their own protection.

BOKY   *(Stands still for some moments, then clutches his head which he shakes dolefully.)*
Les pauvres. Mes enfants. Les petits. Oh they break the heart of their loving Papa Emperor. I open a clothes shop, especially for them. To make sure no one cheats the little ones, I permit no one else to sell the material for their school uniform. They know that their Papa cannot cheat them in his own imperial boutique. I, with my cultured tastes, I condescend to design the uniform myself. My own brothers and nephews operate the only tailors' shops at which the uniforms may be sewn. I have, as you will admit Inspector Brown, taken all paternal measures to protect the little ones.

BROWN   Indeed indeed your Imperial Majesty. No parent could

[27]

have done more.

BOKY   But how do they respond Inspector Brown? With gratitude? No. They demonstrate. They march. They protest. They carry placards. Perhaps they sing songs. Inspector Brown, did my children sing songs?

BROWN   Er . . . we . . . that is, there was report of some singing . . .

BOKY   Loyal songs to their Emperor Papa or bad songs Inspector Brown? Did they sing patriotic songs Inspector?

BROWN   Difficult to say sir . . . er . . . the words were mostly inaudible . . . out of tune sir as . . . er . . . with most children's singing . . .

BOKY   Liar! They sing bad songs about me, their Imperial Papa. Ingrates! Parricides! Bring them to me Inspector. Round them up!

BROWN   They have been arrested already sir.

BOKY   Right here Inspector Brown, right here! At once! *(Brown turns to go.)* No, wait. You! *(Points at random to one of the goons.)* Fetch me the criminals! Bring them to their Papa at the double. Brown, take over the drill. This is a family affair, a—minor—misunderstanding between Emperor Papa and his misguided children. It is my fatherly duty to take the lead in my own person in administering the necessary corrective measures. *(He takes off his jacket and flings it down. Leaps among the squad and does a rapid limbering-up.)* King Herod was right Inspector Brown. We shall emulate his worthy example. Come on Inspector Brown—give us that Lagosian lynch-mob rallying rhythm.

BROWN   *(Snaps into action from a confused state.)* Yes your Imperial Majesty. One-Two-Three—

     O nse mi ki-ki-ki

     O nse me ki-ki-ki

     O nse mi mon-ron-yi

     O nse mi mon-ron-yi

     O nse mi ki-ki-ki

BOKY   *(Alternating between himself stopping and exhorting the squad to greater action.)*

Those are ingrates at your feet. Juvenile delinquents. Future criminals. Little ingrates! Putative parricides! Pulp me their little brains! Wastrels! Prodigal sons! Future beggars! Suspects! Vagabonds! Rascals. Unemployed.

Subversives. Bohemians. Liberals. Daily paid labour. Social menaces. Habeas corpusites. Democrats. Emotional parasites. Human Rightist Vagabonds. Society is well rid of them. They disgrace Imperial dignity. Louts. Layabouts. Now their heads are under your feet. Your chance to clean up the nation once for all. Protect property. Protect decency. Protect dignity. Scum. Parasites. What do you do with parasites? What do you do with fleas! Bugs! Leeches! Even a dog is useful. But leeches on a dog? Ticks? Lice! Lice! Lice! Crab-louse! Stomp! Imperial Stomp! Studs In. Grind! Pre-frontal lebotomy—the Imperial way! Give your Emperor a clean empire. Sanitate. Fumigate, Renovate. *(He clubs the squad right and left to give them encouragement, decimating them until the very last one keels over. Finally realizes he's alone.)* Hey, what's this? A mutiny?

BROWN   Your Imperial Majesty, I think they are not quite as strong as you.

BOKY   Ah yes? Of course. Brown, I want to talk to you.

BROWN   At your service Sir.

BOKY   I have my own lines to the people, and I don't like what I hear. And now these school-children . . .

BROWN   Everything is under control your Excellency.

BOKY   The poor. The poor mustn't go hungry on my coronation day. I hear the hungry have plans.

BROWN   So have we your Excellency.

BOKY   Even during your Civil War in Nigeria, your Chief had a Wedding[12] that was, from accounts right princely. Straight out of the Arabian Nights. And there were no riots! It's peacetime here, so we've no excuse. And it is an Imperial Coronation. We are paying good money for your services. Apart from the good relations that naturally accrue to both our sister nations.

BROWN   You are noble and generous your Excellency.

BOKY   If there is a disturbance, we would of course expel all your countrymen—without notice, without compensation, and without—you.

BROWN   I don't quite understand.

BOKY   *You* would not be expelled. You, Inspector Brown, Special Security Officer loaned to us on Special Duties, you would remain here with us—well, your remains anyway. *(Chuckles.)* Yes your remains—will remain.

[29]

BROWN   Your Excellency, my government would make enquiries.

BOKY   *(smiles)* Our records will show that you left with the rest of your countrymen. Any international Commission would be free to examine our papers and interrogate witnesses. Now send me a fresh squad — to deal with the children. I'll go and change these boots.

(Exit. Brown stares after him, open-mouthed. The Squad drag themselves out, groaning.)

Scene IV

(Anikura's Establishment 'Home from Home for the Homeless')

ANIKURA   *(He is seated at a table, making up his accounts.)* Come in Commissioner I've been expecting you.

BROWN   *(Enters and signals over his shoulders. His men enter, disappear in every direction.)* So you've been expecting me have you?

ANIKURA   Indeed I have. Everyone gets here sooner or later.

BROWN   I see. And apart from that general observation, I suppose that you have done nothing, and you are planning nothing which might lead you to expect a visit from the Law.

ANIKURA   Maybe you can tell me.

(A scream from inside is followed by one of Brown's men backing into the room, fending off blows from a broom wielded by Mrs Anikura.)

DE MADAM   I'll teach you to burst into a lady's bedroom. I'll charge you with assault you piss-pot flat-footed baboon.

(The officer turns and runs for protection behind Brown.)

BROWN   All right Madame, that's quite enough. We do have a search-warrant you know.

DE MADAM   And I know my rights I'll have you know. Nothing gives you the right to burst into my bedroom without knocking.

ANIKURA   All right my dear, I'll handle it. What do you want Inspector Brown? *(The rest of the officers come out one by one, shaking their heads negatively.)*

BROWN   I see. A leakage as usual eh?

ANIKURA   A leakage? What leakage? *(looks up at the ceiling).*

BROWN   Kindly stop beating around the bush. Where are the habituees of this place? They are usually to be found here at this hour. Let's see . . . *(He marches on the table, turns the book round.)* That's right. They've just been in to render accounts. We watched them come in. The place was surrounded and we saw no one leave.

ANIKURA Great detective. Good reasoning Sherlock Holmes.

BROWN *(to his men)* Search the place for secret passages.

ANIKURA Save yourself the trouble. Boys . . .

(What looked like a large stand for clothes and hats suddenly comes alive, like a rotten tree shedding obscenities in human form. The Beggars emerge in all forms of deformity.)

BROWN Good God! What a nightmare.

ANIKURA Take your pick.

BROWN Arrest them all. March them into the Black Maria.

ANIKURA On what charges, pray?

BROWN Coronation preventive measures. We had a hint.

ANIKURA Your good brother Captain Macheath of course.

BROWN That's neither here nor there. Good night. And as for you Chief, better keep your nose clean.

ANIKURA Just a minute Commissioner. *(He gets up from the table, confronts him.)* Are you sure you have enough here.

BROWN Enough? I don't get you.

ANIKURA I mean, these look to me a pitiful small number. A raid should yield something more numerous. Think how the papers will report it. Now, tell me, how many would you really like for a netful. A hundred? Two hundred? Three? I tell you what, I could manage five to six hundred and yet be able to field a thousand mendicants for the Emperor's coronation.

BROWN What are you planning to do Chief?

ANIKURA Inspector Brown, you annoy me. Really you annoy me. On the word of a thief, arsonist, drug-peddlar, murderer etc. etc., you rush here to arrest a few loyal citizens who were gathered here to discuss plans for their own modest participation in the national occasion. They cannot afford Wonyosi, even though, if you'll excuse my saying so, that is a costume for lunatics; nor can they afford champagne—yes, champagne Inspector Brown. Unlike some officers of the law, they can neither afford champagne nor do they have *friends*, friends Commissioner Brown, who fill the corrupt bellies of government officials with champagne. Nevertheless, they have pieced the finest of

[31]

their rags together. They will join the great throng of jubilating subjects. They will wave their little national flags which, as your man may have observed, my dear loyal consort was preparing for them before she was so rudely interrupted.

DE MADAM   I'll sue you for damages too. I believe my sewing machine was damaged.

BROWN   Look Chief . . .

ANIKURA   *(brusquely)* Where is Captain Macheath?

BROWN   How am I expected to answer that question?

ANIKURA   *(resuming his seat)* All right. Go with him all of you. On your way you will find another hundred or two already hobbling to join you in prison. Then, on Coronation Day itself, thousands of the army of the poor will march. Right in the path of the imperial chariot Inspector Brown! Right on to the concourse of princes, presidents, kings and queens, dictators, chairmen, generals and Life Presidents. The Pappal Nuncio will be there, so will the grand Bishops and Imams of the world's great Superstitions. The event will be covered on world-wide television, transmitted to the corners of the globe by satellite . . . Emperor Boky will be very pleased.

(Throughout, the Beggars stand in a huddle, silent. Brown looks at them, shuts his eyes and shudders.)

BROWN   What do you want?

ANIKURA   Macheath. Arrested tonight. Tried in the morning. Shot by noon. Or else!

BROWN   But I don't know where to find him.

ANIKURA   Too bad. *(Resumes his accounts.)*

BROWN   Well, I can't just manufacture him can I?

DE MADAM   You can't be a very good copper if you don't know where to find a notorious public figure like Macheath.

BROWN   This is blackmail.

DE MADAM   Gambling and women. There aren't so many of those haunts that you can't cover in one night.

BROWN   Be reasonable. I just can't go round *hunting* him. I mean, actually *hunting* him! It's bad enough having to arrange his arrest, but to actually hunt him. Be fair Madame!

DE MADAM   *(eyes him scornfully)* All right. *If* I find him for you . . .

BROWN   *(wearily)* I'll do the rest.

ANIKURA   And that's letting you off very lightly. Very lightly indeed. Bursting on the humble dwelling of law-abiding citizens

[32]

just to do the bidding of nefarious gangsters. There are corpses lying everywhere, you don't busy yourself tracking down their killers, oh no. The streets are no longer safe for a poor man, Commissioner Brown. It's a rough world when even the beggar has something to fear.

BROWN   What corpses. I never see any corpses.

DE MADAM   *(sniffs)* I bet you don't. Your friend Macheath always tells you where they are so you can look the other way. Take that Doctor . . .

ANIKURA   And the lawyer . . .

BEGGAR   What of the Musician . . .

ANOTHER   There was that schoolboy . . .

ANOTHER   Even a copper . . .

ANOTHER   And the pastor . . .

OFFICER   My own sister . . .

OFFICER   Entire family wiped out . . .

OFFICER   The trade unionist . . .

ANIKURA   Civil Servants . . .

DE MADAM   That Alhaja . . .

BEGGAR   The pretty trader . . .

ANIKURA   It's a dog's life.

Who Killed Neo-Niga?
(Each chorus is performed to a parody of drill formations by Boky's Goon-Squad while the various social stock characters — the Cash-Madams, Academics, Prophets, Bearded Radicals, Police Detectives etc. etc. mince, snoop, bless, rant, strut in between the drill lines.)

BEGGAR   Who killed Neo-Niga?

BIGSHOT   I, said Sir Bigger
        Puffing on his cigar
        I killed Neo-Niga

Chorus
    All the Army and the Police
    Went a-drilling and saluting
    When they heard of the death of Di Neo-Niga
    When they heard of the death of Di Nu-Neo-Niga
    Tra-la-la-la-la-la-la etc.

BEGGAR   Who caught Neo-Niga?

HIT-MAN   I, said Chief Free-lance

[33]

	Payment in advance
	I caught Neo-Niga
	Chorus
BEGGAR	Who heard Neo-Niga?
ACADEMIC	I, said Professor
	He screamed outside my door
	I heard Neo-Niga
	Chorus.
BEGGAR	Who sold Neo-Niga
CASH-MADAM	I, said Ma Trader
	I'm the Market Leader
	I sold Neo-Niga
	Chorus.
BEGGAR	Who carved Neo-Niga
MEDICO	I, said Doc Morgans
	For his vital organs
	I carved Neo-Niga
	Chorus.
BEGGAR	Who dumped Neo-Niga
OFFICER	I, said the Inspector
	On the A2 Sector
	I dumped Neo-Niga
	Chorus.
BEGGAR	Who saw Corpse Niga?
ALL	I, said the Public
	I'm the New Republic
	I saw Corpse Niga
	Chorus.

(During this chorus, two men cross stage bearing a plain box-coffin inscribed on one side: BODY OF 1001st UNKNOWN VICTIM. They re-cross the stage revealing other side of coffin inscribed: GIFT OF TAI SOLARIN[13] TO A CONSCIENCELESS RACE.)

ANIKURA Who'll solve Case Niga?

(Silence. Bigger puffs his cigar, Army salutes, Police drills assiduously, Doctor sheathes stethoscope, several variations of the 'three brass monkeys'.)

Chorus

    Poor Neo-Niga is a-rotting on the Route A.2
    And a stream of people passing — including you
    And a long stream of cars of the New Republic
    Tra-la-la-la-la-la-la etc.

[34]

(The rhythm changes to a Conga. All join up in a snake-line and exit dancing to the beat of the Conga.)

Scene V

(The Stable. The banqueting-table is still there, bare. Seated around it are the members of Mackie's gang, Mack at the head, Polly on his right, Baba to his left. The solemnity of the scene suggests a parody of a board meeting. A thin file and a heavy ledger, with lock, are tidily placed in front of Polly.)

MACKIE   The meeting is declared open. We will dispense with the reading of the minutes of the last board meeting and proceed straight to business. My dearest wife Polly has brought me the kind of news for which we have devised that contingency plan known under the codename Hideaway . . . *(exclamations of shock and disbelief all round)* It is all too true. My own brother and comrade Commissioner Brown has ratted on me, blackmailed into his perfidy by the rotten devices of Jonathan Anikura . . .

MATAR   You were warned. Messing around with his daughter . . .

MACK   That, is neither here nor there.

MATAR   Isn't it? I knew it would come to no good.

POLLY   Why are you so much against me? After all, I brought him the warning. Would anyone else have done that?

MATAR   Listen to her! If he hadn't gone and meddled with you there would be no warning to give.

DARE   Hm. I always said Matar should have been a lawyer.

MACK   He's more likely to be a corpse if he doesn't shut up soon.

MATAR   You don't frighten me Captain Mack. You've gone and lost us the protection of the law simply because you kept thinking of your own pleasure. *We* are the ones affected. You go into hiding, nice and comfy, you receive your regular cut while we continue to take the risks—without protection!

BABA   Matar, you have a point. Only, don't belabour it so much. The question is what to do?

JAKE   Hear hear. Let's get into Operation Hideaway. Spell it out.

MACK   It's not difficult. You all continue as you are. Simply continue doing what you are doing all along the line.

[35]

MATAR *(looking from one to the other)*
What's this? I don't get it. If Baba takes over the chairmanship from you, that's got to affect his own functions, and so on all down the line . . .

MACK That's what I want to announce, a slight change in Operation Hideaway . . .

JAKE All right Captain, let's have it.

MACK You all forget, we have acquired a new partner . . .*(he ignores the exclamations that spring up all around him)* . . . in the person of my dear wife, Polly. She is the new Chairman.
(A stunned silence, then Matar breaks into a guffaw, followed by all the others except Baba, who remains impassive.)

DARE All right Captain, now you've had your little joke . . .

MACK It is not a joke. Polly takes over.
(They all turn to stare at Polly, then at Baba.)

JAKE Well, what does Baba say about that?

BABA *(after a pause)* Well, it seems to me she is better at figures than I am. This is not the old days you know. We are not just hoodlums, we have investments in banks and cooperatives. All those things are rather complicated.

MATAR I don't care. *I* am not taking orders from any woman.

MACK Perhaps you wouldn't even take orders from Baba if I wasn't around. Maybe you are even thinking you should run the outfit in my absence?

MATAR I wasn't thinking that but, now you mention it, why not? At least I wouldn't do such a dumb thing as go into matrimonial alliances which endanger the firm.

MACK *(half-rising)* Shut up!

BABA *(restraining him)* Let's all be calm. Matar, look, the trouble with you is that you simply don't understand how complex our operations have become lately. We no longer bury our proceeds in the wall you know, sneaking through some smelly latrine to go and take out a wad or two for the week's pocket-money. We invest them. We buy shares in businesses. We follow the rise and fall of stocks and shares on the market. We have a cut in the lucrative foreign exchange racket, that is, our partners are some of the most respectable men around. Now, Mack could handle a lot of that himself. You'd be surprised how much of that business is conducted over the table at the Casino, or in

[36]

the exclusive Club of Top-Twenty, of which Mack was made a special Visiting member. You have to have class to get into that kind of company.

MATAR *(sneering)* And she's got class?

POLLY You're right I haven't. *(She has picked up the ledger and, swinging it spine first, catches him forcefully at the base of the head.)* Take that you insolent bastard! *(Matar pitches forward, stunned.)*

MACK *(looking around)* Any other objections?

JAKE Not me.

MACK Dan?

DARE I see we've got a real Chief.

BABA I always knew she had spirit. Let's get on with business Captain.

MACK Take over my dear.
(They change places.)

POLLY *(jerking her head at Matar)* Somebody wake him up.

JAKE Allow me Chief. *(He gets a glass of water, lifts up Matar's head and dashes the water at his face. Matar splutters and revives.)*

MATAR What . . . what . . .

POLLY Now sit up. Pay attention and listen. Before we get to real business there are one or two things which must change around here. First, your comportment.

JAKE Go easy Chief! Comportment, what's that?

POLLY The way you bear yourselves, your manner of dressing, of addressing people, your general appearance. Right now it's disgusting. I noticed it first on my wedding day. You have to improve.

DARE *(groans)* I don't understand. What's wrong with us as we are?

POLLY Nothing when you were merely hoodlums. From now on, think of yourselves as businessmen. You must change with your new status.

DARE Do you mean we are not going to be able to do the odd job here and there, knocking off this and that . . .

JAKE Just to keep in training you know. Businesses go bust all the time and then we'll need to fall back on the old pickings.

POLLY That brings us to the next point. We have to do some recruiting . . .

MACK Polly, are you sure you aren't moving too fast?

[37]

POLLY   Mack my dear, if you'd moved this fast before now, my
father would not have been in a position to run you out of
town. I want you to be walking the streets again soon,
with your head held high and no one daring to touch you.

MACK   Sweetheart, I knew I was making the right choice. Go
ahead.

POLLY   I've picked up a few tips here and there from my father's
way of running his business. We could use them here.

MACK   *(gesture of surrender)* As you please my dear.

POLLY   Tomorrow, you'll all go to the tailor and get measured for
new clothes. Lace of course. In a week's time I don't want
to see any of you appear in public in anything but lace.
Blue lace.

MACK   Wait a minute, wait a minute . . .

POLLY   Don't worry dear, I know what I'm doing. You Mack,
when you come out of hibernation, you'll re-enter society in
a new outfit no one in these parts has ever seen.

MACK   Well, won't you tell me what it is?

POLLY   I'll do better than that. I'll show you. *(Takes out a parcel
from her briefcase.)* It's the latest craze from home. The
very latest. No one has ever seen it in this country.
*(She unwraps the parcel, unfolds the dress in it to reveal
an outfit which closely resembles some form of lace
'agbada' stuck together in bits and pieces.)*

MACK   What on earth is that!

DARE   Christalmighty!

POLLY   Watch your language Dannyboy! Don't swear before me.

DARE   I beg your pardon ma'am. But seriously, what is it?

POLLY   It's the one and only—Wonyosi. The only fashion in the
right circles. This one costs some five hundred dollars a
yard.

DARE   Five hundred dol . . .!

BABA   So that's the famous Wonyosi.

POLLY   When you wear this at home, it's a sign that you've
arrived.

MATAR   Or going places? Like our Captain.

POLLY   Oh, you are now with us are you?

MACK   My dear, I'll do most things for you but . . .

POLLY   Try it on please.

JAKE   Yeah, go on Captain, let's see if it suits you.

MACK   But Polly, you wouldn't really foist on me some cast-off
from your father's wardrobe would you now? Not even the

[38]

most desperate beggar would wear this.

DARE   Oh come on Captain, put it on.

MACK   *(sniffing it)* Well, it smells brand-new . . .

POLLY As if I would dream of putting you in second-hand clothing.

BABA   Captain, wear it. I know the stuff, honest, I mean, I've heard of it. The best people wear it at home. The very best.

MACK   Yes, but . . .

BABA   You've got a right sharpish missus here Captain. The more she gets into things, the more I see what a sharp business mind she's got.

MATAR Now what are you talking about?

BABA   I think I see what she's up to. We are expanding all the time right? And we've got all those business associates at home. Well, what happens when one of our home partners comes here? He meets our Group Chairman here, our Captain Mack, all togged up in Wonyosi. Well, what is that visitor going to be, you tell me that?

DARE   Impressed. Baba's right.

MACK   Is that the idea Polly?

POLLY Of course. You in Wonyosi, your business advisers here in blue lace, seated at a table like this. Our partners will start talking in millions . . .

MACK   All right. I recognize business logic when I hear it. I'll go and try it on.

DARE   Good Captain.

POLLY And now gentlemen, while Mack is changing, let me bring you up to date on the way business has been shaping lately. Acting on my advice, we have bought a thousand shares of Igbeti Screwall Investments Ltd.

JAKE   Never heard of them.

POLLY A new multinational corporation with special holdings in developing countries. Launched from Nigeria of course, after the discovery of a rich lode of marble in some obscure village. Today it is personally, repeat, personally backed by at least fifteen African Heads of State.

MATAR *(straining to read the ledger)* How much did that set us back?

POLLY Practically all we have in fluid cash. And there is no need to twist your neck trying to sneak a look at the accounts. *(Pushes the ledger at him.)* All you have to do is to ask to read it.

MATAR *(hotly)* I wasn't trying to sneak any look . . .

[39]

POLLY Read it. All members of the firm are free to inspect the books anytime.

MATAR *(pointing)* Is that it?

POLLY That's it. Any questions? You may pass it round the table.

MATAR Pretty steep eh? Though I must say the profits are equally high.

POLLY In three months, higher than you all ever made in three years of robbing and smuggling and killing and pimping.

MATAR *(pushing the ledger back)* I've no questions.

POLLY Are you sure? Take another look. Nothing there strikes you as rather funny?

MATAR Oh ease off on me lady. Did I make any imputations? I say I'm satisfied.

POLLY Then let that be a lesson to vou. Listen very carefully, and I mean all of you. The figure against those thousand shares is inflated four times.

MATAR What!

POLLY Yes, four times. Because you see, although there are only one thousand shares written down, we actually paid for four thousand shares. Five hundred went to Commissioner Brown. Five hundred went to a mistress of Emperor Boky, another five hundred was bought in the name of one of his latest bastards. Five hundred went to the Director of Prisons and the final thousand were personally handed to the Deputy Chief Justice of the Empire for re-distribution if and as how he thinks fit. Any questions?

JAKE Ma'am, you mean we distribute three-quarters of everything we get?

POLLY You are learning fast Jake. And the lesson of it for you all is that, while the books are always open for inspection, only I *know* the book. I distribute as I think fit and I report back to the firm when I think it necessary. And I want no silly questions from any ignorant sods who don't know their left from right in the new business.

DARE Ma'am, if we are going into high finance, I am quite happy to leave it all to you. Especially with profits shooting up as high as that.

JAKE I call it as-tro-no-mi-cal!

BABA I told you all.

JAKE A financial genius!

MATAR *(protesting)* I still think we ought to know something of . . .

[40]

DARE   *(singing)* For she's a jolly good fellow . . . *(The others join in, excepting Matar. The singing is interrupted suddenly by a loud whistle. They freeze.)*

POLLY   Commissioner Brown?

JIMMY   *(dashing in)* They are practically on the doorstep. Tiger Brown and the Emperor's elite raiders.

JAKE   The Y Squad?

JIMMY   No less.

MATAR   *(disappearing)* See you all!

POLLY   Mack! Mack!

MACK   *(putting out his head)* What's going on?
  (Jake and Dan Dare also vanish.)

POLLY   Tiger Brown, and the Y Squad.

MACK   Already?

POLLY   Hurry Mack, hurry!
  (Mack emerges, with only one leg in his new trousers. Stumbles and falls. Polly hauls him up. He struggles to find the other leg with his foot as a crash is heard.)

MACK   Mack!
  (Mack abandons the effort to complete his dressing, hops out on one leg.)

BROWN   *(followed by squad)* Fan out! Find him!

POLLY   Were you looking for someone Commissioner?

BROWN   Don't imagine I didn't see you behind the clothes-rack in your father's place. But fair's fair. It was only reasonable I should allow Mackie his fair warning. Or . . . was I thinking that it would make it easier to find him by simply following you? *(Sententiously, with a sigh)* Oh the complexity of human motives!

POLLY   And I thought you were his friend.

BROWN   I still am. But your father drives a hard bargain. Blame yourself and Mackie for getting me into this mess. *(Looks around)* Yes, board meeting I suppose? *(He stands expectant.)*

POLLY   *(pushing the ledger to him)* There are the accounts.

BROWN   I don't need to read that. I trust you. *(pause)* Well?

POLLY   *(still pretending to misunderstand)* Oh, of course. *(Brings out a piece of paper.)* Sawleg Dudu—you can have him for that murder on rue St. Augustine. Mack says we can provide three witnesses who caught him in the act. And Shoo-Be-Show—he's getting too showy. Our boys have

[41]

got to keep a low profile in the new line of operation. Shop
him for that rape of the nun behind the Sacred Hearts'
Hospital. Pasco Kid had the nerve to do some intimidating
on his own account—remember that Manager of the
Supermarket Chain Stores who wouldn't lodge a complaint? Well, that's Pasco Kid. He's running a protective
racket on the side and letting people think he's boss. Well,
Mack *is* the Boss. Out of sight or actively engaged, he's
going to remain the No. 1. Take Pasco Kid for the
burglaries at St Lazarin. We'll give you some merchandise
from there decorated with his full set of fingerprints . . .

BROWN   I bet you will. *(Pulling out a piece of paper in turn.)* And
when do you propose to give me the felon whose charge
sheet includes *(reading)* murder of two shopkeepers and
four tourists, 30 burglaries, 23 street robberies, arsons,
attempted murders, forgeries, perjuries etc etc not to
mention the seductions of two sisters under the age of
consent . . .

POLLY   *(heatedly)* That's a lie!

BROWN   Which one?

POLLY   Mack never seduced anyone?

BROWN   A-ah, so you do know who did all the other things. Got
you. Now skip all that business of the fall-guys. *(holding
out his hand)* We were actually discussing book-keeping
before we got—sidetracked.

POLLY   Not while Mack is in danger.

BROWN   Business is business. The rest of the firm still need
protection.

POLLY   I'll discuss that after Mack is out of danger.

BROWN   My dear girl, I run a lot of expenses.

POLLY   Oh you are really heartless. To think that you and Mack
were once comrades-in-arms.

BROWN   *I* am heartless? Oh, that's rich. Just look at you, taking
over the business as if you were born into it. Calm as a
cucumber. Where is that sweet innocent girl whose
wedding I attended it seems only yesterday?

POLLY   Where is the palm-wine that frothed so sweetly yesterday?

BROWN   Drunk. Imbibed.

POLLY   Drained. Soured. Turning vinegary.

BROWN   But stronger in spirit content, right?

POLLY   That's Nature for you.

[42]

The Song of Lost Innocence

POLLY   In case you're trying to puzzle out my transformation
         I'll let you all into some secret information
         Once I was one like the wilting lily of the valley
         Who didn't have to sweat to fill her little belly
         Then something else began to fill my little belly
         A fruit of love or, say, of frolics in the alley
         And to teach what life is all about
         There's nothing like a new life hereabouts
         And your breadwinner on the fast way out
         Soon ends your period of self-doubts
         If women seem weak, it's because they prefer to avoid
         too much bother.
         You know of my father; you've yet to learn of De
         Madame, my mother
         Heard of 'Attack Trade'?[14] While Mackie and Brown
         were ripping the insides
         Of foes; Mother was dodging the bullets and ripping off
         both sides.

(Enter Chorus of Women, led by De Madam)

WOMEN   Forward Ever! Backward Never
         Attack! Attack! Attack! Attack!
         Trade is the stuff of life
         War is the stuff of trade
         Cash has no after-life
         Shuns company of the dead
         Come, your scruples sever
         Act a little clever
         When you've no friend or foe
         Business is never slow
         You don't believe me?
         Ask your masters the Big Powers
         While the poor wretch counts his last hours
         Trade is boom-time in Megalopolis
         London. New York. Moscow. Paris.
         How to sell to Left and Right
         Yet prove you're doing right
         Weapons for each bloody fight
         Man, I tell you it's out-of-sight!
         So why condemn me? So why contemn me?
         I'm just a pretty-trading, high-risk, low-profit, quick

[43]

turnover, one-act, Mother Courage, troop-comfort, friend-and-foeing sunshine-rainshine Attack Trader!

POLLY   If men are beasts, shan't we ensure they cannot eat us?
One day it's love, the next they raise their fists to beat us
They throw you over when beauty goes and strength is sapped
And you stare at the shreds of eternal love you had mapped
When, eager to bear his seed, to spawn and raise his heir,
The future filled with music, roses and eternal care.
But to teach you what life is all about
There's nothing like a new life hereabouts
And your breadwinner on the fast way out
Soon ends your period of self-doubts
Whatever the male can do, the female can do even better
Don't rely on your tears, when push comes to shove from the rotter
Mackie is different I swear, but a girl must protect her future
If a girl doesn't learn from her mother, experience will prove a harsh teacher.

(The Chorus of "Attack Trade" is repeated, with Brown's Officers returning and joining in, feigning shot and dying. The women march over them, stop to empty their pockets, take off their watches and carry on business throughout the chorus. Curtains close and lights come on in the auditorium with the Women offering those wares among the audience along the aisles.)

END OF PART I

PART TWO
Scene VI

A Whore-House in Bangui, also known as Play-Boy Club

MACK *(entering through a window)* Verily verily is it spoken, Hell hath no fury like an aggrieved father-in-law. I escaped the clutches of the law by seconds only, driven from the promise of a honeymoon bed, yet grateful for the warning of my faithful, ever-loving wife concerning the desperate machinations of her father. Well, I must seek solace for momentary deprivation. *(whistles)* Though I must say, it's pretty hard on a newly-wedded bridegroom to be separated from his beloved. *(Places two fingers in his mouth and whistles.)* One thing about Sukie, even if she is with her millionaire Sugar-Daddy, she'll find a way to dodge him for old Mackie. For a few minutes anyway . . . I don't believe in pressing my claims unduly.
(A door opens slightly and a face peeps out, followed soon by the rest of the body.)

SUKIE *(coldly)* What do you want?

MACK *(looks round, unbelieving)* Who?

SUKIE Do you see any other skunk in the corridor?

MACK Why Sukie, it's me Mack, your Mack.

SUKIE I can see it's you Mack. Smooth Mack. Dandy Mack. Wonyosi Mack. *Polly's* Mack. *(Turns round and slams the door.)*

MACK Oh dear, I do believe she's heard about Polly. *(Suddenly he listens. Sure enough, sounds of sobbing are heard from behind the same door.)* Ah, I couldn't quite believe that such a sweet natured girl would turn heartless tigress because of a simple marriage. *(He goes to the door, opens it cautiously, looks inside.)*

SUKIE *(from within)* Oh Mackie, how could you break a poor girl's heart so.

MACK I can explain everything . . . *(The door is shut on the rest. Enter De Madam. Looks up and down. Enter a Very Rich Gentleman.)*

[45]

VERY RICH GENTLEMAN	Oh there you are. You must be the Madam.
DE MADAM	*(instantly suspicious)* How come you know me?
VERY RICH GENTLEMAN	Well, it's a simple matter of deduction. You are a little . . . er . . . if I may say so, a little too old to be one of the girls, so you must be the Madam.
DE MADAM	And who gave you the right to mistake me for a common brothel-keeper? I'll ask you to keep your distance and maintain respect for the wife of Chief Jonathan Anikura, Chairman of highly successful Groups of Companies.
VERY RICH GENTLEMAN	Oh, I most awfully beg your pardon. But you yourself, I thought you said . . .
DE MADAM	I am known as De Madam. A very different and respectable kettle of fish from the *Madam* with whom, if I may so presume, your business lies. And now if you'll excuse me . . . *(Goes off.)*
VERY RICH GENTLEMAN	Oh dear, oh dear, very touchy lady. Ah, that looks more like it. *(He sees Jenny who has entered with bucket and mop, broom etc., going to do the rooms.)* Excuse me young lady . . .
JENNY	You want the office don't you? Straight along the corridor, turn right, first room on the left. The Madam is always there.
VERY RICH GENTLEMAN	*(tips her with a note and chucks her on the chin)* Most obliged my dear child. *(Jenny lets the note hang in her hand, looks after him as he goes off. Bitterly.)*
JENNY	Do have fun!
VERY RICH GENTLEMAN	*(Turns round, a leer and a wink.)* I was assured this is the place for it. *(Waggles his fingers and goes off.)* *(Jenny puts down her pail and mop, sings the Song of Jenny Leveller.)*

Jenny Leveller

Sodom and Gomorrah
Will seem quite paradisial
When this whorehouse comes to trial

On that soon-to-be tomorrow
You in your golden villa
Will know this life for real
In that cup of no denial
As I shout Hip-hip-Hurrah!

But the hand that passes sentence
Will not descend from heaven
There's a girl who cleans the linen
Smeared in spunk of moneyed wantons
It's the girl you tip the tuppence
Who scrubs from nine to seven
She'll watch you slowly riven
On the rack named DECADENCE.

Your hat sir, your umbrella
Hope you had a very good time
Mind the stairs now as you climb
Lest you break your bloody neck sir
There's a horde who've marched from far
Just to fill your mouth with grime
And roll you in your slime
As I shout Hip-hip-Hurrah!

Nor Sodom nor Gomorrah
Did ever see such panic
As when I end the picnic
Yes, this shabby Cinderella
Would have lit your last cigar
For it's time to face the music
Of the crowd you've driven frantic
Hear them shout Hip-hip-Hurrah!

DE MADAM *(re-entering)* I'm not getting the right cooperation. *(Sees Jenny.)* A-ah. As a student of human nature, admittedly not in the same league with my husband the Chief, I think I know an ally when I see one.

JENNY *(pointing to the door through which Mack disappeared)* In there. Her patron millionaire is due any moment now so you won't have long to wait.

DE MADAM Oh Jenny my dear . . . *(feeling inside her purse)*

JENNY *(showing her the note)* No need to bribe me. Someone else has paid me for doing my job, so take your account as settled. *(She takes out her key, opens the door into another room and shuts it behind her.)*

DE MADAM   Well, well, the cheeky hussy. *(Sounds from Sukie's room brings her back to caution. She sprints down the corridor and hides. Mack re-emerges, buttoning up.)*

SUKIE   Hurry now, he'll soon be here.

MACK   Later tonight then.

SUKIE   Make it before one in the morning. He usually leaves at 12.

MACK   Okay, okay.

SUKIE   Oh Mack dear do be careful. Are you sure you wouldn't rather hide in the wardrobe? At least with me I know you're safe.

MACK   I might fall asleep and start snoring.

SUKIE   But he's deaf and half-blind I tell you. If you fell in through the door he'd still think it was a rat or something.

MACK   *(appears to consider it)* No. Anything could happen. He might detect me and then I'd be forced to kill him.

SUKIE   Well, that's never bothered you much has it?

MACK   This one would. Against my principles — killing the goose that lays the golden egg.

SUKIE   *(chuckling)* Oh Mackie you are a one. You know how to make a girl laugh. Where will you hide meanwhile?

MACK   I might visit the Casino . . . oh, which reminds me . . . I am rather short. Can you . . .?

SUKIE   But the Casino Mack! Everybody will see you there.

MACK   Only the rich. And they don't read the *WANTED* column of newspapers.

SUKIE   Are you sure . . .?

MACK   Oh shut up and give me what you have. You want your Sugar to come in while we stand here yapping?

SUKIE   *(sulkily)* Oh all right. You always get in a temper when you set off to gamble. *(Reaching inside her bra.)* Which do you love more Mackie? Me or gambling?

MACK   Both, silly. See you first thing after midnight. *(saunters off)*

SUKIE   Bye Mackie. Do be careful.

  (She watches him disappear. Immediately De Madame appears.)

DE MADAM   Well, Sukie?

SUKIE   I haven't seen him.

DE MADAM   I know you haven't seen him dearie. But when is he coming back?

[48]

SUKIE How do I know, when I haven't seen him?

DE MADAM Sukie, think of what he's done to you. Think of what he's done to us. That's our only daughter. We bring her up, treat her right, we plan great things for her and see what happens. He's going to take her to the gutter with him.

SUKIE My Mackie is a fine gentleman, he's not taking anyone to the gutter 'cause he ain't there himself.

DE MADAM You still aren't using your head. Polly's a minor. But, all right, she's also a wife . . .

SUKIE Wife! Liar. He never married her.

DE MADAM Oh, is that what he told you?

SUKIE He swore to me. Oh I admit he's fond of her. He's fond of every woman and I can't say I blame him. He is quite good-looking you know.

DE MADAM Stop being so scatter-brained. He married her. MARRIED! And if you don't believe me, ask Commissioner Brown. He was present at the banquet.

SUKIE *(beginning to break down)* And he swore to me . . .

DE MADAM Don't snivel. Just listen carefully. If Macheath cops it, that makes her a widow, right? But she's also a junior. So that means she really couldn't get married without our consent—Chief Anikura's that is. With Mack gone, we become her legal guardians. Don't worry, the Chief has some nifty lawyers among his lot and they've worked it out. Now you know that Mack is not a poor man . . .

SUKIE Mack not poor! Business has been bad for him. His associates rob him blind! He has to borrow money from me to keep going.

DE MADAM Exploitation! That's what it is—Exploitation. He exploits you, you soft-headed ninny. Next to the Chief my husband in person, your poor Mack represents the largest shareholder in all the businesses of New Ikoyi. Don't take my word for it—ask Commissioner Brown. Mack pays him 25 per cent of everything he gets, you ask Brown how much he gets and work it all out from that.

SUKIE *(discomfited)* He's just taken every last penny I had on me. He's going to spend it gambling.

DE MADAM Gambling! See? That's what he does with the money you earn the hard way. Putting up with that toothless, hairless, sightless, spunkless old goat. When are you going to grow up? Now let me finish what I set out to say. With Mack gone, his properties revert to his widow, which means that

[49]

as her legal guardians we control them. You know Chief Anikura, he never breaks his word. And he says one-quarter of that is for whoever helps us nab him.

SUKIE Oh Mack . . .

DE MADAM When does he come back?

SUKIE I couldn't betray him. Never. Oh, here comes Old Sugar now.

DE MADAM Sukie . . .

SUKIE I won't betray Mack. *(Going, pauses.)* Well, just the same, for whoever is interested, Old Sugar always leaves at midnight. Goodnight. *(sniffs)* Poor Mack. *(Enters room.)*

DE MADAM *(grinning)* In this world of treachery, it is good to meet such loyalty in a working girl.
(A wizened old man, nearly bent double, taps with his stick along the corridor, peering closely at each door.)
This way Romeo. *(Pulls at him sharply so that he is almost catapulted through the door.)* And be sure you're out of here by midnight.

Scene VII

PRISON. Mackie's cell.

DEE-JAY It's done. The great bandit Macheath is in gaol, betrayed by one love too many. The law has taken its course, proving most vibrantly that no one is above it—Hear, hear!—except of course you happen to wear the right kind of uniform—Three Hearty Stripes—or—Pip! Pip! Pip! Hurray!—Oh man I'm flipping again—let's get back to the great man. What are his thoughts as he stares at the broad back of his goaler through the thick bars of his cell?

MACK Do you fancy my clothes?

DOGO *(Turns round and studies him for a few moments.)* Well sir, now that you bring the matter up, I've been meaning to ask you sir, were you trying to climb through barbed wire when they caught you?

MACK Ha ha very funny. Very very funny. You don't understand how ignorant that makes you.

DOGO *(he comes closer)* No, seriously sir, when they brought you in I thought what a pity you had to ruin such good lace. I like lace you know. But this one looks as if the police dogs

[50]

and barbed wire had been fighting over it.

MACK   Well, take a closer look. That's the latest fashion back home. This one cost over five hundred dollars a yard.

DOGO   Is that god's truth? *(Puts his hand through the bars and feels the cloth.)* You may be right sir. It feels expensive.

MACK   Of course I'm bloody right.

DOGO   It will never catch on here mind you. The Faranse[15] prefer that business-like two-piece thing they wear—except for the been-tos[16] of course. You can't separate those ones from their three-piece collar and tie affair.

MACK   Would you like it?

DOGO   Which one? Me wear a three piece?

MACK   No, this one. My wonyosi.

DOGO   Oh, is that what it's called?

MACK   That's right.

DOGO   Hm, well, I must say one might get used to it. But right now . . .

MACK   *(impatiently)* Use your imagination man. Christ, that's why people like you never get on. Get used to it . . . who asked you to get used to it! Didn't you hear what I said? this dress cost over five hundred dollars a yard!

DOGO   Well, I still don't see what you are getting at. Even that price takes some getting used to wouldn't you say sir?

MACK   *(holding his head)* You'll never make it! You're only fit to be a prison warder.

DOGO   Maybe. I thank you for the insults. It's the privilege of a man who is at the point of death to speak his mind.

MACK   Don't! Don't use that word.

DOGO   Oh, I'm sorry sir. I wasn't trying to say anything painful. I'm a religious man you know. I never hurt a man when he is down.

MACK   Nor help him up I suppose. Well then, listen again. How many yards do you think have gone to make me this thing.

DOGO   You mean the whole complete?

MACK   Everything. There is even a cap—I lost it while trying to escape.

DOGO   Hm, I think there are some 10 yards involved in all of that.

MACK   All right, we'll say 10 yards. Multiply 500 by 10.

DOGO   *(gives a slow long whistle)* Five . . . thousand dollars!

MACK   Now convert that to CFA and work out for yourself how many thousand francs I am wearing on my person right at this moment.

[51]

DOGO *(pop-eyed now)* The things a man could do with that amount!

MACK You have a family?

DOGO Two wives, seven children.

MACK And of course they are well-fed, they wear good clothes, they lack for nothing . . . in short, you don't need money.

DOGO Who doesn't need money!

MACK Maybe you even have debts.

DOGO How did you guess?

MACK Now, answer, do you want this wonyosi or don't you?

DOGO Well . . . it seems hardly fair to er . . . I mean, it's like robbing a corpse — oh, I am sorry.

MACK Never mind. Let's get down to business. If — what we have agreed not to mention again were to happen, I would have no use for it, right? So, take it. Now!

DOGO But what will you wear?

MACK *(snapping)* Yours yours! Don't you understand? We change clothes. For that you get five thousand dollars in wonyosi convertible currency. You can sell it in the Nigerian quarter — you know it don't you? — New Ikoyi. It's even worth your while to take a special trip to Nigeria — ask for sick leave or something. The latest news is that the stuff has been banned, so it will cost even twice as much. You are not above a little smuggling are you? I'll give you a note to those who will show you the ropes . . .

DOGO *(who has finally taken it in)* I am beginning to see your little game sir . . .

MACK And about time too. What do you say?

DOGO It's a big risk for a man, a family man like me, to take.

(Noise off, like a steel gate opening.)

MACK Someone's coming. Think quickly man!

DOGO I'll go and see who it is. *(Goes off.)*

MACK That one is a dead loss. A born pauper. All timber up here. You can't bribe a man like that. To be bribable you've got to be imaginative. That's why the cleverest men are the most corruptible.

DOGO *(runs in)* It's Inspector Brown. A thousand dollars down.

MACK *(puzzled)* What?

DOGO A thousand dollars down. I prefer cash to Wonyosi, or whatever you call it.

MACK Where would I find such a sum?

DOGO Not where but when. Not would but must. Before midnight. *(Dashes off.)*

MACK I could have sworn . . . just shows how wrong you can be. No doubt about it, my countrymen have inherited the earth.

BROWN *(Off.)* At ease Dogo. And out! Stay out of earshot. *(As he enters, Mack turns his back.)* Oh Mack, don't do this to me. You are breaking my heart.

MACK *(not turning)* It is generally accepted that a man, in his last hours on earth, should be afforded the privilege of choosing his company.

BROWN I did all I could Mack. You know that. And you had warning . . .

MACK Warning? Not from you. You never had the slightest intention of warning me.

BROWN Polly warned you. I saw her behind the clothes-stand. I saw her run out and, even after trailing her to your meeting-place I went through the motions of gathering up the Elite Squad just to give you time.

MACK Very impressive Commissioner Brown, very very, impressive. In that case, I am not here at all. I am not in prison. I was never captured by you, taken to court, tried on the evidence you provided. I have never been condemned to death, oh no. I am enjoying the pleasures of my normal haunts, not held here at the pleasure of His Imperial arsehole, awaiting execution.

BROWN That's it Mackie. That's exactly what did it. Why did you not leave town altogether? Why go to the brothels where you are so well known. Whose fault is that?

MACK *(Turning round, draws himself up proudly.)* That question, Commissioner Brown, illustrates all too clearly, if at all any illustration were needed, what a mundane, pedestrian, low-born, hoi-poloi soul inhabits your carcass. You actually expected that I Captain Macheath would give up my normal routine of pleasures because some flat-footed rookies were after me? You have never yet—and there have been times when I have wondered at the inequality of our friendship, times when you have sunk so low that I have hesitated to acknowledge you in public—but never till now have you achieved such an all-time low. I see you now on a par with the sewer-rat in a skunk-hole and implore you to remove your obnoxious presence from my sight . . .

[53]

BROWN (*dabbing at his eyes*) Oh Mack please . . .

MACK . . . unless of course you have come here with some practical suggestions about getting me out of here!

BROWN No Mack, I cannot.

MACK I thought not. Go. No, stay. Have you thought out every possible way?

BROWN I haven't slept a wink or eaten a bite for thinking.

MACK For God's sake man! You couldn't get up any good ideas even on a full belly and a good night's sleep, yet here you are starving your stomach of food and drink and your brain of rest, and you imagine you can think straight? I am well and truly lost!

BROWN Oh don't say that Mackie.

MACK Why not? You have some rescue plan?

BROWN Mackie, Polly your wife is outside. She wants to see you.

MACK Fine. Very Fine. I ask you for a rescue plan you tell me my wife wants to see me. If that's the best you can do, send her in. Go on, go and fetch her. At least she can muster ten times your intelligence.

BROWN (*going*) Oh Mack, you simply enjoy torturing me.

DOGO (*dashing in*) A thousand dollars, before midnight. What do you say?

MACK You're an expatriate aren't you?

DOGO Of course. Same as you, from Nigeria. That's why I'm doing it. I wouldn't take such a risk for anyone. But blood is thicker than water.

MACK Or cash eh? The money has nothing to do with it.

DOGO I have to take risks. The money must be in my hand by midnight.

MACK We swop clothes and I get out?

DOGO That's the idea isn't it?

MACK My wife is coming in. She'll arrange it. (*Dogo dashes off*) Amazing how animated his face has become in the past few minutes. Maybe it's the other way round. The smell of money endows the dumbest Nigerian with instant intelligence.

(*Enter Polly, followed by Brown.*)

POLLY Oh Mack!

MACK Leave us copper. I need some private discussion with my wife.

BROWN I can't do that Mack. You are not even allowed visitors — officially you know.

[54]

POLLY The rest of the firm are outside too Mack. They said they have come to pay their last respects.

MACK Don't! Don't say such thing. Christ! People only say that of a corpse already lying in state.

POLLY Forgive me Mack, I am so sorry.

MACK How could you be so insensitive!

POLLY I wasn't thinking, I'm sorry. I just blurted out what they said.

MACK Oh, that's what they said was it? It goes to show you. Positive thinking is not for that lot, oh no. Are they thinking of how to get me out? Not on your life. They are concerned only with paying their last respects. Brown, I want to see those bastards.

BROWN Oh no, oh no no no, you can't hold a convention here.

MACK I want to see them I said. You're getting very obstructive aren't you Brown? Just remember there are papers and things which could be released to make things a little uncomfortable for you.

BROWN You wouldn't blackmail an old comrade Mack.

MACK I can and I will, if you don't let those men in. Is it asking too much of you? If you can't help me out of here at least you can help me put my affairs in order. I propose to hold a board meeting. Here!

BROWN All right, but you must promise to . . .

LUCY *(Off.)* Get out of my way you mutton-headed bum. I'm his wife and I demand to see him . . .

MACK Christ, Lucy!

POLLY Lucy?

BROWN What's going on? *(runs off)*

LUCY *(Still off.)* I saw that bitch come in here. If she can go in so can I.

POLLY Who *is* Lucy Mack?

MACK Oh er, you mean Lucy. Well, er, you have to er . . .
(Enter Lucy heavily pregnant, followed by the gang, in uniform lace. They carry neat portfolios. Brown pants in behind them.)

MACK *(quickly to Polly)* She's a bit mad, I remember her now. You'll see for yourself.

LUCY *(Pulls up short at the sight of Polly. She circles her scornfully, then makes a spitting noise.)* So that's the Lady of the grand airs she gives herself. They tell me you think you are married to Mack. I hear it all over town, now let me

[55]

hear it from your own mouth.

POLLY Who is this cow Mack?

LUCY Ah good. That's very good. I knew all that varnish would soon come off when it came to the point. Not quite the fancy bitch you try to pass off on those who don't know better eh? Get her out of here Mack, tell her you want to talk to your wife. Alone.

POLLY His wife!

THE GANG His wife.

POLLY Mack, is this woman your wife?

MACK I was going to tell you; she is actually the daughter of the prison governor.

POLLY Well well Mack, you certainly move in the best circles.

MACK Polly, let me talk to her a little. She's mad, quite mad, but I can calm her down. I know about her through her father you understand?

POLLY Well you can talk to her in the presence of your wife I hope. You have no secrets from me have you Mack?

MACK No no, but listen. Don't you understand? She is the daughter of the prison governor, the PRISON GOVERNOR Polly! Now you see why we've got to humour her.

LUCY Is she going or not Mack?

MACK Yes dear, of course she's going. Brown, talk to Polly outside for a moment will you.

(Polly allows herself to be led off by Brown, protesting.)

POLLY Mack . . .

MACK Trust me. *(She goes. The Gang is about to follow.)* As for you lot, start thinking about how to get a thousand dollars together.

MATAR What for Captain?

MACK What for, you frog-face? Maybe to paste all over the walls of my cell. Maybe to wipe my arse with since prisoners don't get supplied with toilet paper. Maybe just to stuff down your greasy throat you double-crossing bastard. I said start working out how to get a thousand dollars raw cash together, so get started. I want it within the hour.

BABA Right boss, leave it to us.

JAKE But we don't have that sum.

DARE The time is too short.

BABA Come on boys, let's go and think it over. We may come up with something.

MACK You'd better. Unless you want to see me full of holes by

[56]

tomorrow night.

MATAR Oh come on boss, who would wish a thing like that on you? *(Grins evilly)*
(They troop off.)

LUCY Oh Mackie, look at the mess you've got yourself into. You promised you would lay off those whorehouses didn't you? Now you've gone and got yourself betrayed by some cross-eyed bitch who can only capture to herself a half-blind scaly lizard that can't even get it up any longer.

MACK I am really surprised at myself you know Lucy. But you know, old habits die hard. Anyway, it's you and you alone I've ever loved. That I still nurse a passion for the old slap-and-tickle doesn't mean a thing. After all, what's a man without his ruling passion?

LUCY I couldn't love you without one.

MACK You understand me Lucy, for once a man can truly say I have a wife who understands me.

Song of "The Ruling Passion"
(Mack and Lucy)

What is your ruling passion?
Being without's not in fashion
Since Alexander Pope observed it
Discriminating men have served it.
It will save you and me a lot of time
To know how to please you in your prime
So come out with it
Let's get on with it
Tell me your ruling passion.

Don't pledge yourself to ration.
Is it lace that brings you elation?
Was it on your account they banned champagne?
Tell the truth and we'll counter-campaign
Man should indulge in what he pleases
Who cares who calls them social diseases
Don't sit on the fence
You'll go all tense
Tell me your ruling passion.

I tell you this bloody nation
Is getting above its station

[57]

It turns on you its voice of prudery
If you get an orgasm from bribery
Corruption's the oil that greases
The national wheels and smoothes the creases
Of the body politic
So don't be romantic
Tell me your ruling passion.

Now sex always stays in fashion
An egalitarian passion
When question papers succumb to leakage
And the student is foaming with rage
When the dumbest suzie obtains a first-class
Remember that sex transcends all class
So hitch up your star
And hitch down that bra
Tell me your Ruling Passion.

Is it Wealth that makes you bash on?
And throw to the winds all caution?
If the Money Ritual demands your wife
Why hesitate — it's only a life
And think of the parties you can give
When money flows all hearts forgive
So don't be so squeamish
Serve her to your Fetish
Tell me your Ruling Passion
Lay down your Rules of Pash!

LUCY   But Mack, what about that bitch who was here? It's all over town she is your wife.

MACK   I won't lie to you Lucy. You know me too well and you understand me. Of course I had something to do with her. She's attractive and I am always seducable.

LUCY   I knew her type the moment I set eyes on her. She's the seducing type all right.

MACK   Yes, she went straight for me. Threw herself at me. I didn't resist. How was I to know she would go round town saying I'd promised to marry her? From there it was only one short step to actually claiming I've married her.

LUCY   The trollop! I knew you couldn't commit bigamy.

MACK   I wouldn't dream of it. But Lucy, let's not talk of her. The

problem is getting me out of here tonight. Otherwise . . .
(He makes a firing noise.)

LUCY You mean they will actually shoot you.

MACK Unless you help me Lucy.

LUCY But what can I do?

MACK I think I can get out of the building itself. The guard is open to ideas. It's the outer gates that may give a little trouble. Can you get the key to the warders' entrance from your father's room?

LUCY It isn't possible Mack. He carries the whole bunch around with him.

BABA *(re-entering with Polly)* Captain, we've sent the others away so we can tell you what we've been up to. They might raise objections — that Matar especially — over the expenditure. You needn't worry about that thousand dollar you see . . .

MACK *(excitedly)* You hear that Lucy? Can't you do your own part.

LUCY *(shaking her head)* You know you wouldn't need to ask me twice if I could. I know it can't be done.

POLLY Hm. A broken reed.

LUCY And just what is that supposed to mean Madam?

POLLY Just what it said. A broken reed. Obviously Mack finds he cannot lean on you.

LUCY *(patting her stomach)* Can't he? If he wasn't doing more than leaning on me, how do you think that got there?

POLLY Mack, is what she is saying true? Is that really yours?

LUCY You think I put it there myself?

MACK Er Polly . . . listen . . .

POLLY Is this woman carrying your child Mack?

MACK Is this a time to worry about details like that? Go after the thousand dollars and get me out of here!

DOGO *(Strolls past as if on patrol.)* Time is running out sir.

MACK You heard him.

BABA Is it past visiting time?

MACK *(wildly)* No, no. He's talking about the deadline for his bribe.

POLLY When you come out Mack, where will you go? I mean, who is your wife?

LUCY What a foolish question!

MACK When I get out of here Polly, I leave town, not so?

POLLY *(persistent)* Who will you send for? Who will you rely on?

[59]

Who do you call wife Mack?

LUCY Stop pestering him with silly questions.

POLLY Well, it's simple. The firm has taken in hand arrangements for your escape. I stuck out for you Mack. I rushed to give you warning, yet you left me Mack, and went straight into the arms of that whore Sukie, when you should have been fleeing town. She betrayed you. Now we're trying to get you out again. If we succeed, are you going to get trapped again in the dugs of some other cow like that?

LUCY *(Leaping at her.)* Are you referring to me you shit-face? *(They fight. Baba tries to separate them and gets flung aside. In the struggle, Lucy's 'pregnancy' slips down, Polly gains the upper hand, kneeling over her.)*

POLLY Well well, what's this then? *(She slips a hand under Lucy's skirt and brings out a bundle. Just then Brown comes running in.)*

BROWN What's going on? Oh. Is it a boy or girl?

MACK *(chuckling)* The prettiest baby bundle I ever saw.

BROWN Come on you trouble-maker, out you go. *(Seizes her under the arms.)*

LUCY Let me alone.

BROWN Come on. And I don't care whose daughter you are. I'm responsible for the well-being of this prisoner. *(He drags her out, assisted by Dogo.)*

MACK Now you see for yourself Polly. Are you now convinced? She is quite mad.

POLLY Well, I am not convinced Mack. *(Presses gently on her stomach.)* And mine is for real.

MACK What! Already?

POLLY So you've got to come out. I don't want my child's father to end up shot in public like a common criminal.

MACK Now that's the kind of talk I like Polly. The thousand dollars is assured then I take it.

POLLY Better than that Mack. It's been put to use already. And more than a mere thousand.

BABA We've been doing some hard work Captain. That's what we really came to tell you. You are almost as good as free.

MACK Hey, that's not good enough. I don't like the sound of that word, almost.

POLLY Don't worry Mackie. First, we've got a stay of execution. Signed by the Deputy Chief Justice in person. *(Hands him the paper.)*

[60]

MACK   Hot dog! I knew those Igbeti Screwall shares were worth a tidy sum on the international market.

POLLY   And you've won a re-trial. Or appeal. He'll decide what to call it when you appear before him tomorrow.

MACK   I can't take it all in yet. To have miracles pouring down among prison walls, with a veritable angel, my own Polly dishing them out right and left . . . it's too much. Give me your hand to kiss. *(Pulls her hand inside the bars and kisses it all the way up to the shoulders.)*

POLLY   By noon tomorrow, you'll be a free man.

BABA   But ten thousand dollars poorer.

MACK   A sound investment Baba. *(He is studying the document.)* But tell me Polly, who thought up this loophole, this secret society business?

POLLY   The Justice himself of course.

MACK   It's genius. Pure genius.

DOGO   *(patrolling)* Time is running out sir.

MACK   Hey you. Come here.

DOGO   Sir? You called me sir?

MACK   Yes, you beanpole, come here. What did you say just now?

DOGO   You haven't forgotten the thousand dollars have you sir? You've less than 30 minutes to deliver.

MACK   Does your mother yet know what a blubber-bottomed pinhead-brain orang-utan of a son she delivered? Back on your beat, loser!

POLLY   Oh Mack, isn't it nice to see you have lost none of your spirit.

BABA   Yeah, the Captain is always the Captain no matter the circumstances.

MACK   Well, I'll tell you something, I can't say I've been very fond of these particular circumstances. I'll be glad when I'm far from them.

POLLY   Don't worry my dear, it won't be very long now. If you knew how much I've worried.

BABA   The prospect was revolting Captain. And you in that new get-up. I mean, there are already enough holes in it . . . oh I'm sorry.

MACK   No, I don't mind references now that it's all over. Too much of a good thing is bad—aesthetically speaking.

POLLY   Only one more night my dear and then . . .

MACK   Back to the life of ease . . . I can't wait. God, what a hole!

[61]

POLLY   And oh Mack, promise me, promise me you won't do any foolish thing that would bring you back in here. No treacherous women, no dangerous adventures. Let's go legitimate like the bigger crooks.

MACK   Of course my dear. Trust your Mack. One thought of my near escape, even the very thought of prison . . . *(shudders)* Ugh, words cannot express the sense of degradation, humiliation etcetera etcetera. No, words are most inadequate, so why don't I just sing you the song I've composed here to pass the time. I've given it the title "It's the Easy Life For Me" because, looking from the inside to the world outside, that's what everybody seems to be after—a life of ease—at the expense of somebody else of course.

POLLY   Naturally.

BABA   Quite so.

It's the Easy Life for Me
[Sung by Mackie]

Have you seen those workers daily jostling
To catch a bus to beat the factory deadline?
And the pregnant mother wedged with elbows
Barely dodging those haphazard blows
You'll claim the boss is also on the breadline
The "go-slow" has wrecked his daily hustling
Well, a whole day in an air-conditioned car
Is sweeter than one hour in over-heated air.

Chorus: Explain the smugness on the face of the chauffeur?
            He knows that at the bus stop life is even rougher.

Have you been to the hospital lately
And seen despair on faces in the line
Insolence from clerks lolling on the table
A waiting-room that smells worse than a stable
You'll say the rich are also laid supine
Diseases fell them though their life is stately
Well the rich can telephone for private cure
While for an aspirin the poor must long endure

Chorus: Explain the joy-on-the-face of the Medical Apprentice?
            The Medical Council has voted for Private Practice.

[62]

Did you go to the cathedral the other Sunday
And hear the bishop on the theme of pain?
Suffering is sent to make a fellow great
Fighting with rats for gari[17] in a garret.
Bullshit! Let riches fall on me like rain
And keep your starving greatness any day.
A life of ease is what a rich man knows
Glory is cold when the wind of hunger blows

Chorus: Explain the beggar's rapture hustling by the mosque
He's chewing fleshy nuts while the prisoner gets the
husk.

Scene VIII

DEE-JAY   And now, fellow expatriates, we proceed to show you that
even the greatest men have their moments of doubt. True
greatness comes however from the methods applied to
resolve doubts, and if such doubts prove impossible to
resolve, from an ability to transfer such doubts unto
others. Once again, the scene is the headquarters of Home
from Home for the Homeless.

ANIKURA   *(He has been standing still, chewing his lower lip.)* A dirty
trick. Just the kind of low-down skunk-stunk trick to
expect from a so-called Captain who does not even understand what it means to talk of *(palm over his heart)* "my
honour as an officer and a gentleman".

DE MADAM   It only worked because he has the police on his side.

ANIKURA   The police hm? Well, maybe we can rake up something
higher than the police.

DE MADAM   But dearie, the police are in charge of the law.

ANIKURA   The question is not who's in charge but who makes the
law. The question is always—who's the law-giver? *(A
knock on the door.)* That will be Colonel Moses now.
Right, let him in.

JIMMY   Enter the Capo di Capi. He's all yours Chief.

ANIKURA   Stay! And bring in the others. I asked them all to stay
around. Colonel Moses has to see us for himself *(Jimmy
gives a piercing whistle. From every direction the Beggars
begin to limp, crawl and otherways ingratiate their way in.)*
Stop! Stop it! Do you think you can milk one centime out

[63]

of the Colonel here? He'd as soon shoot out your empty sockets as give you money for a false eye. Sit down, act normal. I brought you here as evidence, as witnesses, Get up! Get up! Where's your manners? Have you found the Colonel a seat yet? Telling you to cut out the beggar-stuff isn't the same as asking you to lose your sense of precedence. Can't I ever teach you anything? If you can't act servile before the military you haven't yet learnt the art of begging without seeming to beg, right?

BEGGARS *(As they scramble to find Moses a chair.)* How to beg without seeming to. Lesson Nine.

ANIKURA Now that's better. Squat where you are and occupy as small a space as possible — the Army's here.

MOSES Oh please Chief . . .

ANIKURA No, if *you* please Colonel, only if you please. Now please, I want you to take a look. Take a good look.

DE MADAM *(stage whisper)* Do you think he might like a drink?

ANIKURA Of course. Colonel, May I present . . . my consort. De Madam is how she is known among ours.

MOSES I am honoured madam.

DE MADAM *We* are Colonel, *we* are. Now what shall I offer you as refreshment?

ANIKURA Open that champagne we've been saving for the Emperor's coronation . . .

MOSES Oh no, it's banned. Oh, of course I'm away from home. No, no matter what, I'm still an ambassador for the nation.

ANIKURA The champagne my dear. *(Madam Anikura goes off.)* Captain Macheath had six magnum at his wedding and Commissioner Inspector of Police Brown didn't say no. Now what's Brown but a mere law enforcer? You by contrast, Colonel Moses are a law-giver. If champagne is okay for a mere enforcer, and a bent one at that . . . ah there you are my Colonel *(Madam Anikura enters with three glasses of champagne which are taken by Moses, Anikura and herself).* Your health Colonel.

MOSES Yours Chief. *(He looks round uneasily as he drinks. The Beggars are staring unblinkingly at him.)*

ANIKURA Gazes down rookies! *(All eyes are immediately lowered.)* You must forgive them my Colonel. It isn't so much that they are ill-mannered for staring, as that they can't forget what they were, or what they hope is in store for them. Too impatient you see. And yet, the sight of this cham-

[64]

MOSES   *(clearly embarrassed)* I er . . . I . . .

pagne, drunk so fraternally by you, me and my consort, serves to stimulate them along the path of dilligence in scholarship. Take a look at them Colonel. Take a good look at them.

MOSES   *(clearly embarrassed)* I er . . . I . . .

ANIKURA   Naturally, with their guards dropped, with their play-acting suspended you cannot believe your eyes. Well, your eyes do not deceive you. Stand up Professor Bamgbapo.

BAMGBAPO   *(suavely)* Colonel Moses, surely you remember me.

MOSES   What! Not Professor . . . I mean, our Chairman of the Mining Corporation.

BAMGBAPO   At your service.

MOSES   But what are you doing here? I mean, you were not retired. I . . . I . . . yes, you were even commended for . . .

BAMGBAPO   Yes, I am still on active service Colonel, both at the University and in the Ministry of Mines and Power. But right now I am on sabbatical from the university and on study leave from the Ministry.

MOSES   But surely, I mean, why . . .

BAMGBAPO   Sabbatical, *and* study leave. As you observe, I am undergoing a refresher course. All perfectly in order.

MOSES   A refresher course in what, Professor?

ANIKURA   Do sit down Professor, I'll take it from there. Now Colonel, how do you think our good friend here bagged his Professorship? And how do you think he went on to bag the Chairmanship of one corporation after another? And how, let me ask you, am I prepared to bet you 500 Naira to the entire day's takings of Anikura's Army of Beggars that, shortly after his Refresher Course, he will also bag the chairmanship of the National Haulage, Air-Freight and Shipping Lines? Now you tell me that.

MOSES   *(shaking his head)* I think I'm going crazy.

ANIKURA   Not at all. Boys, read him the First Commandment.

ALL   He who begs, bags.

ANIKURA   He who begs, bags. *(They all burst out laughing.)*

BAMGBAPO   Colonel Moses, how do you think I developed such a persuasive style of sucking up to the Army boys. Well, I suppose to some it comes naturally. At first I fooled myself I was a natural beggar. Fortunately, one of Chief's talent scouts spotted me in time. I was invited for special training.

DE MADAM   *(pouring)* A little more champagne, Colonel.

[65]

BAMGBAPO *(self-assured)* I haven't done too badly have I Master?

ANIKURA Down! Gazes down! Right down! Crawl! *(They all obey. De madam refills the champagne glasses.)* Boots, boots! (They begin to lick Moses' boots, noisily. He flees.) Now take a good look Colonel. Take a damned good look. Does that bunch look like a secret society?

MOSES What!

ANIKURA Well, decide for yourself. Does that look like a dangerous, secret society?

MOSES I'm afraid I don't . . .

ANIKURA Understand? I'll explain. This establishment, this High Institution of Learning, of Research, this Beneficient Society for the Relief of Burdened Consciences, this . . . oh, it's too much! It's too much Captain.

MOSES What is it Chief? Tell me.

ANIKURA *(Goes nearer, booting the Beggars out of his way. They crawl back to their positions.)* Did you not follow the Appeal Session of the case of Macheath? We were denounced. An enemy of state, in prison for multiple murders, arson, forgery, fraud, bawdry, blasphemy, rape and seduction and other unmentionable acts, this social fiend, deservedly condemned to public execution tomorrow got some traitors to swear to an Affidavit denouncing my Home from Home for the Homeless as a secret society — just to escape hot perforations.

MOSES But why? What has it to do with you?

ANIKURA *(puffing his chest)* We did it. He was convicted on our evidence. But the Appeal Court has now decided that evidence was worthless. Macheath's appeal was granted and he was set free to roam the streets an hour ago.

MOSES *(getting up recites:)* Since I came to Centrafrique as Legal and Security Adviser, whose brief, apart from matters of Internal Security, embraced the reform of the present reactionary and colonial legal system inherited from the French, the formulation of new Statutes in consonance with the forward-looking spirit of a modern imperial age, I have done my best to ensure the independence of the judiciary at all stages. I have been gratified to find that the Emperor himself — we might as well give him his full title now *(looking at his watch)*, it's less than 15 hours to go — I was saying, I have been very gratified that the Emperor has accepted this principle of the independence of the

[66]

judiciary. I cannot now go back and recommend any in-
terference in the carefully laid-out judicial processes.

ANIKURA It does you credit Colonel. Still, he who makes can break —
that's an even older adage. You made the law. Even if you
won't exactly break it you can bend it a little.

MOSES And how do you recommend one does that?

ANIKURA A tiny decree, back-dated of course, abolishing the right of
appeal from your Special Tribunals.

MOSES *(going)* Excuse me.

ANIKURA You think that's fair do you? You advised the Imperial
Decree on secret societies didn't you?

MOSES A short cut for dealing with subversives. All subversive
movements are by nature secret. The stability of the
regime had to be protected.

ANIKURA But you've gone and given a convenient weapon, not just
to our enemy, but to the Public Enemy Number One. He's
escaping the local Bar Beach Show thanks to you. Mr
Law-giver, do you call that justice?

MOSES The law is ineffectual unless it guarantees the security of
the ruler. In the process, it is not unthinkable that a minor
criminal or two might escape the noose.

ALL Minor criminal!

MOSES Well, good night. Stay out of sight tomorrow. The streets
must be free of any unsightly appearance. *(As he exits, a
scream is heard from outside. Colonel Moses backs inside
while Jimmy dashes out in the direction of the noise.)*

ANIKURA What the hell . . .!
*(Jimmy returns dragging a squirming prophet Jeru with
him.)*

JIMMY Look what I found.

ANIKURA Well, well well, fancy meeting you here. Spying as usual I
suppose?

JERU Changing sides if you want to know. *(He keeps his
frightened eyes on Colonel Moses.)*

ANIKURA *(a big guffaw)* Changing sides. That's rich. And from
which side to which?

JERU It's simple really. One of my er . . . little flock came to
inform me that a uniformed man was seen entering your
headquarters. Counting by the stars and pips and
whatever, it was my informant's opinion that the officer
was of no less a rank than that of a Brigadier.

ANIKURA Colonel actually. Well, what about it?

[67]

JERU   What difference does it make? Even a corporal would do for Captain Macheath. All he's got is the police. If you've got the Army on your side . . . well, at the very least it puts his fate in the balance. I don't like hanging there with him.

ANIKURA *(to Moses)* See? What a friend. What a Holiness. Still you haven't told us why you had to yell out like that.

JERU   Oh, I recognized him that's all. He took the skin off my back the other day. Well, night to be more accurate. But I recognize him all right.

ANIKURA What's all this about? He's a legal adviser; he's not a Commissioner Brown prowling the streets you know.

JERU   *(stubbornly)* It's him all right.
        (The Beggars have become more alert, begun to take interest.)

BAMGBAPO Did you say at night?

AHMED   Allah, it's him!

MOSES   I . . . er . . . I think there's some mistake.

JERU   Mistake! His men held me down on the bonnet of my car — you know my Volvo 264 of course, bought for me by my grateful congregation. My driver overtook his car and that annoyed him, so they chased me, held me down on the bonnet while he applied a koboko to my back. Twelve strokes in all.

AHMED   Yes, it's him. Chief, you know that culvert under the bridge where we sometimes pass the night. They came in one night and dragged us all out. I remember him saying he was getting rusty and needed to keep in shape. Eighteen strokes apiece!

BAMGBAPO I wouldn't have believed it of you Colonel Moses. So it was you at the Night-Club Bistingo! Chief, Look! *(He shows him his back.)* I had just come out from the Bistingo — I go there to relax after the day's practicals, you know. I began negotiations with this . . . er . . . prostitute. All work and no play you know . . . Well, he sat in his car . . . I didn't see his face you see. But he sent his driver to go and bring the same girl. I told the Driver to go to hell. The next moment I was down in the gutter. The driver took my neck at the back and pressed my face into the muck. He came out of the car and lay into me with his swagger-stick. I fainted, Chief.

MOSES   *(coldly)* It was someone else. If you fainted, how could you say it was me?

[68]

BAMGBAPO	Because of what you said. They were the last thing I heard before I passed out. You said, Ha, that's cured a little of my nostalgia for good old Lagos.
MOSES	I tell you, you are all mistaken. I who have shaken hands with the Emperor-to-be, could I descend to such a level?
AHMED	It's sheer profanity Chief. The Koran approves begging.
ANIKURA	My beggars. My boys. My prize pupil. *(He collapses in a chair.)*
DE MADAM	Mind your heart dearie.
ANIKURA	My prize pupil! The humiliation.
JERU	And a holy man in my prophet's habit. Laid out on the red-hot bonnet of my Volvo 264, flaggellated like the two thieves on either side of the Cross . . .
ANIKURA	Shut up you double-dealing profaner! *(Sips from the glass offered him by De Madam.)* Law-giver Moses, did you really get back into your old habits at the expense of my boys?
MOSES	A mistake. It can happen to anyone.
ANIKURA	*You* laid a hand on my boys! Do you know how much I pay your counterparts here for protection? Do you?
MOSES	Please, don't make such an issue of it.
BAMGBAPO	You bet *I* will. I'll make a report of your conduct when I return home. I can reach ears higher than yours you know. You'll be recalled and court-martialled. A disgrace to your uniform. *(Moses smiles smugly.)*
ANIKURA	He'll like that. Ho ho, he'll like that. Look at him! He knows nothing will happen to him from that direction. I could report him to Folksy Boksy who likes to have a monopoly in the matter of stamping the life out of vagrants and children but, Boksy might actually give him a medal. He's getting no younger you know, so he doesn't mind a little help from specialists. No, what we'll do is . . . Let me think! *(He strikes his thinking pose.)*
JERU	If I may make a suggestion.
ANIKURA	Shut up! *(A few seconds silence.)* I have thought. Where is Tako the Law?
ALATAKO	Chief?
CHIEF	Boky is our target. Think of a way of getting him bad with Emperor Boky in person. Frame him or something. Some act of *lese majeste* — that's French for imperial infra dig. Maybe Commissioner Brown can come into it . . .
MOSES	*(frightened)* Look here . . . perhaps I can explain. You

[69]

	have to remember I was not properly briefed.
ANIKURA	Not properly briefed . . . that's the black man for you. He arrives in a strange country and starts skinning his own countrymen . . .
AHMED	The Koran says it's blessed to give.
ANIKURA	Colonel, meet a fellow professional of yours, A. G. Alatako, whom I've assured will beg his way to the rank of Attorney-General in less than three years. He will prove such a beautiful beggar that the Sharia[18] Courts will compete for him to be their President. Relax Moses. Alatako here is going to devise a beautiful frame-up for you. Maybe he will furnish proof that the Nigerian government actually sent you here to sabotage his coronation. He'll believe us — our people have been making radical noises lately.
ALATAKO	The notice is short your Worship. Could one plead for an adjournment?
ANIKURA	Not much time. if he is to get the Emperor to sign that Retroactive Repeal of Right of Appeal, track down and recapture Captain Macheath, tie him to a stake and execute him before tomorrow's Coronation pageant . . .
ALATAKO	I'll need the latest newspapers from home. And a few moments er . . . your Lordship . . . yes, just a short adjournment to prepare my brief.
ANIKURA	Court Adjourned! Jimmy, fetch that bundle of papers which came with the consignment of second-hand velvet from Alhaja Bosikona. Class, while we are waiting for the court to re-convene, what about a little song on the noble art of begging. Dee-jay?
DEE-JAY	Why not the anthem itself Chief. It's a high point in the *deroulement* of events I think. I would recommend The Beggars' Anthem at this point.
ANIKURA	I bow to your professional judgement.

The Beggars Anthem

> To beg is to bag
> Not, is to lag
> Behind most successful men
> Is a history of fulsome mien
> It's not such a shame
> If you wish to make a name
> To learn how to butter up
> How to be a sucker-up

[70]

I know a famous type
Whose seeks for favours ripe
When a Big Shot calls him on the phone
He would fling down his body prone
He turns lizard clown
His head up and down
And recites his favourite formula:
Idobale ni mo wa. [19]

When a soldier sets on you
And beats you black and blue
Don't bother to protest
It's no worse than Soro manhood test
And the louder you can beg
The less your knees will sag
And remember to say Thank you sah
Lest he show you yet more power.

Pride has a price
Too heavy for the wise
The excess weight of opulence
Is balanced by benevolence
We fill a social need
Take the stigma out of greed
Have you money, power or place to spend?
The beggar is your friend.

ALATAKO   Chief, we have him! *(Flourishing a newspaper.)*
ANIKURA   Are you sure?
ALATAKO   Try me, Chief. I propose to hoist him on his own petard.
ANIKURA   The court is now in session!
ALATAKO   With your permission your Lordship, I wish to present this document in evidence!
ANIKURA   Is it admissible? Speak, law-giver. *(Moses remains silent.)* Silence means Consent. The document[20] is admitted in evidence. The document is headed Ref. No. B.63214/Vol II/258 Federal Ministry of Establishments dated 15th August, 1970s. It is hereby admitted.
ALATAKO   I shall now proceed to cross-examination.
ANIKURA   Stand by Jimmy. This is not the United States, Colonel Moses, where you can get away from speaking the truth by pleading the Fifth Commandment.

[71]

BAMGBAPO   Amendment, Chief.

ANIKURA   What?

BAMGBAPO   Amendment, amendment. Not commandment.

ANIKURA   Are you sure?

BAMGBAPO   My C.V. boasts some five solid papers on the subject.

ANIKURA   Are you suggesting they made up ten Amendments to the Ten Commandments?

BAMGBAPO   Chief, we are talking about the Fifth Amendment.

ANIKURA   Thank you. Which is what you Moses, are not allowed to take. If he does Jimmy, you know what to do. This is not a savage country where people pretend to obey the Ten Commandments but make one Amendment so they can frustrate all ten. Proceed.

ALATAKO   Colonel Moses, do you admit that you are the Army Legal Adviser to the current regime in the old homeland etc. etc. *(Moses remains stubborn. Jimmy moves to a position directly behind him.)*

MOSES   I am not the Legal Anything.

JIMMY   *(arm poised for a blow)* Do I . . .?

ALATAKO   No, not needed. Colonel Moses, do you understand legal arguments?

MOSES   I was trained as a lawyer.

ALATAKO   Good, good, we make progress. Would you say, Colonel Moses, that you are the most senior member of your profession who holds an army rank?

MOSES   What does that prove?

ALATAKO   *(indulgently)* You have to answer the question.

MOSES   *(shrugs)* I suppose so.

ALATAKO   I am satisfied with your answer. And now Colonel Moses, pay strict attention please. Do the following names and dates mean anything to you? Mushin Riots 1970; Ugep Village, 1975; Epe Riots, 1975; orile-Agege, January 1976; Kalakuta Feb. 1977; Shendan, Plateau State, June 1977; Enugu, September 1977 . . . I could go on for ever your Worship . . .

ANIKURA   No please don't go on for ever. He is the one who would like to hang on for ever. Terminate his agony.

ALATAKO   As your lordship pleases. I have yet another question for the accused. Did you have a hand in the drafting of the Secret Society Decree for Centrafrique?

MOSES   Don't you agree that secret societies are an evil menace, a cankerworm in the fragile solidarity of the nation, a danger

[72]

to national security.

ALATAKO Absolutely, absolutely. I implore the court to take special note of the loyal sentiments of the accused. Condemned or not by this court, they should be passed on to his bosses.

ANIKURA Pray proceed.

ALATAKO With your permission your Lordship, I would like to offer the already tendered document B.63214/Vol II/258 to the accused. Do you recognize it?

MOSES Yes that's the government directive to . . .

ALATAKO Kindly limit yourself to the simple answers Yes and No. Yes-no?

MOSES Yes.

ALATAKO Do you admit to having a hand in these definitions of a secret society?

MOSES I certainly will not deny it. If you had any idea the harm which secret societies . . .

ALATAKO I assure you Colonel Moses, this document does you credit. I congratulate you. It is one of the most inspiring and cleansing documents of our time. Now be good enough to read your first definition of a secret society.

MOSES *(reading)* A secret society is defined to include any society "whose membership is not known or made public".

ALATAKO I am grateful to the witness. Not known. Not made public. Now Colonel Moses, kindly tell me what the organization which you represent had to report about the identity of the culprits in the military-civilian riots which we have had the displeasure of enumerating before this court. Of the criminal gang involved in the burning down of villages, assault, rape, murder etc. etc. your Organization blamed, in 1970 . . .

ALL Unknown soldiers.

ALATAKO In 1971?

ALL Unknown soldiers.

ALATAKO 1972?

ALL Unknown soldiers.

ALATAKO 1973?

ALL Unknown soldiers.

ALATAKO 1974?

ALL Unknown soldiers.

ALATAKO 1975?

ALL Unknown soldiers.

[73]

ALATAKO 1976?

     ALL Unknown soldiers.

ALATAKO 1977?

     ALL Unknown soldiers.

ALATAKO 1978?

     ALL Unknown soldiers.

ALATAKO 1979?

     ALL Unknown soldiers.

ALATAKO 1980? Oh, wait a minute. Are we ahead of time?

ANIKURA While you are getting back in time, let's have the Ballad of the Unknown Soldier.

DEE-JAY Gee, I'm sorry, haven't got all the sound-effects for that yet. We tried to get the real thing you know, the sound of smashed windscreens, bones crunching, koboko descending, violated daughters, screaming students, you know, the usual stuff. But the recording machine got smashed.

ANIKURA What! Who dared?

     ALL Unknown soldiers.

     (The Beggars break into the "Unknown Soldiers" Dance, full of contortions, limping and groaning.)

ANIKURA Ha! All right, let the law take its course.

ALATAKO Unknown soldiers. Not known. Not made public. Major Moses, I put it to you you are part of a secret society.

MOSES Nonsense, you can't persuade the Emperor with that. All soldiers have their names on the government payroll. What's so secret about that?

ALATAKO Colonel Moses, I must impose upon you once more. Kindly read the last paragraph of definitions of a secret society in Document B.63214/Vol II/258. Loud please.

MOSES *(Reads with Emphasis.)* . . . whose members are under oath, obligation or other threat to promote the interests (legitimate or illegitimate) of one another and come to one another's aid *under all* circumstances, without due regard to merit, fair play and justice, to the detriment of the legitimate expectation of non-members.'

ALATAKO Thank you Colonel Moses. Your Worship, I refer you to the widely-reported details of the burning down of the Kalakuta Republic. I refer you to the even more recent incident in Kano where a whole batallion of soldiers, because one of them was knocked down, barricaded the streets, violated all passers-by, totally innocent passers-by,

[74]

maimed, looted, burnt and intimidated all and sundry without a consideration of the *merits or demerits* of their grievance. And I quote again portions of the definitions of a secret society . . . , formulated by Colonel Moses, Law-giver Extraordinary in person—I quote . . . whose members are under oath, obligation, repeat, obligation, or other threat to promote the interests (legitimate or illegitimate) of one another and to come to one another's aid *under all* circumstances.' . . . 'Under all', your Worship, being a qualification actually underlined by Colonel Moses and his brink-tank . . . I continue, quote . . . 'without due regard to merit, fair play and justice, to detriment of the legitimate expectation of non-members. Non-members. That's us, your Worship. Us. I beg to rest my case.

(Applause from all the Beggars, they crowd round him, slap him on the back, shake his hand, Cries of 'Tako the Law' etc. create a din.)

ANIKURA *(banging a bottle on the table)* Order! Order in my court damn you! Order! *(Silence is gradually restored. Some seconds after silence Anikura still sits, pondering.)* Hm. Class, certain issues of constitutional dimensions have been raised. Such as—are we, or are we not being run by a secret society? Colonel Moses, be a friend of the court and come to our aid. What say you?

MOSES Well, I don't know. What do you want me to say?

ANIKURA Oh nothing, nothing. But you are an officer and a gentle-man, that means, a man of honour. If you find . . . and as an enlightened man you are not one to refuse the validity of arguments . . . If you discover how easy it is to be accused of being that which you are not, and you happen to know also of others who are being victimized through the accusation of being what they are not—and with even less reason! Damn it! 'Come to one another's aid?' Look at them! These rats would take the last morsel from each other's mouth if they could get away with it. No Colonel, there is nothing secret about this society. Can you say the same of yours? If we were to contact Commissioner Brown with our evidence—you represent rival organizations and Emperor Boky is a very hasty man, very hasty indeed. For him *any* secret society represents a personal threat. What say you sir?

[75]

MOSES   *(suddenly resolved)* Enough! *(All eyes turn towards him.)*
Macheath . . . shall die. *(He marches off as one who means business.)*

DEE-JAY   *(Commentator's Excited Voice.)* . . . And it's Civil Guard, Civil Guard ridden by Baba Yaro heading once again for a winner — a full length ahead of Kijipa his nearest rival and only other real contender worth bothering about. Boy, what a horse! That's not to say he's having it easy all the way. Sunny Boy on Kijipa is making it quite a race. Trying everything to get the last ounce out of that horse, really laying on the whip. No, no question about, Sunny Boy isn't a quitter, he's using the whip more and more in desperation but no, he really isn't in the same class as Baba Yaro. That game little jockey has ridden Civil Guard with beautiful teammanship. He seems to have that uncanny horse intelligence, knows just when to give Civil Guard a second wind, when to restrain him a little, knows when to take him all out. They are coming round the final bend now and the position is exactly the same, Civil Guard one length ahead. No doubt about it, what Baba Yaro has is strategy. Sunny Boy seems to depend entirely on the whip to bring the best out of Kijipa. Only some ten lengths away from the tape, Baba Yaro really coaxing the last effort out of his mount, pulling away a further head and . . . that's it! Civil Guard the winner by nearly a length and a half. And what a superb finish. What a pair! What a team! Baba Yaro on Civil Guard, winner of the Imperial Stakes . . . *(Volume trails off.)*

ANIKURA Of course! Coronation races. The Imperial Stakes. After him Jimmy! After Colonel Moses. That's where he'll find Macheath. Hurry up the lot of you. You should be at the races begging. Find Macheath and keep him under close watch until Colonel Moses gets there. Better not fail!

DEE-JAY   . . . and the moral of that astonishing contrast of styles is this — You can whip a horse to water, but it takes the know-how to make him drink. *(Winks broadly.)* End of message. Oh, you don't mind do you? You have to get it in whenever you can. One of these days it might actually sink in — Fat chance!

Scene IX

(Directly after the Dee-Jay's comment, the band strikes up the tune of 'Who Killed Neo-Niga', this time in a brisk, 'Putting-in-the-boot' tempo. The Dee-Jay follows them in, doing a yet inaudible commentary into a hand-mike. Balloons float down from every direction and streamers fly through the air. Shouts of 'Hail Boky!' 'Long live the Emperor' 'Long live the Imperial Family', 'Long live the Dukes, the Duchesses, the Earls and Marquises' 'Long live Africa' 'Hail the Dawn of a New Age'. Then to the steady beat of 'Neo-Niga', Boky's goon-squad enter chanting 'Vive, Vive, Vive L'Empereur', 'Vive, Vive, Vive l'Empereur . . .' They are nearly across the stage when a voice sings out:)

VOICE   Who CROWNED De-Niga?

(Dead Silence. The squad-leader brings them to an on-the-spot movement, looks round him, searching for the singer. Suddenly he sees the culprit, screams 'There!', warms up the squad for action with the first steps of the Boot Stomp and launches them after the victim. They disappear off-stage. Dee-Jay comes on stage.)

DEE-JAY   Yea-eah man, go get him! Yeah folks, on this beautiful dawn in Bangui, it's fun-and-games as usual, only more of the same, more colour more splendour, more pageantry. And Captain Macheath is going to lend his own bit of colour to the occasion by bleeding through several holes to the delectation of the populace—men, women and children, the aged and crippled, from all walks of life . . . oh here they come! They've come from distant parts of the country and—oh yes, the scramble has begun for ringside seats.

(An ice-cream vendor cycles past.)

VENDOR   Ice-cream! Keep cool with your favourite Ice-cream. Special coronation flavours. Imperial vanilla. Caramel Bonarparte. Gateau Imperatrice . . .

DEE-JAY   *(holding out a mike)* Hey brother, how many ice-creams you hope to sell today?

[77]

VENDOR Are you kidding? Do you know how many schools have declared a holiday so they can watch the execution? Man, I'm already sold out!

DEE-JAY There it is. It makes your heart glow to see such a crime-busting, righteous people. They HATE sin, and they are going to see that the criminal gets his right royal deserts.
(Enter a Patient, swathed in bandages, on crutches. A Nurse follows him with a drip-bottle still attached to his arm.)

PATIENT Stop nagging me! I tell you I'm going to watch this one even if it kills me.

DEE-JAY *(holding out mike)* Excuse me sir . . .

PATIENT Of course I believe in public executions.

DEE-JAY Well, that wasn't really what I was going to ask you sir.

PATIENT Then it ought to be young man. I can see you don't know your job. And I tell you something else, before they shoot them, they should drain their blood and put it in a blood-bank.[21] Then upright lawabiding citizens like me can gain something at least from their worthless existence.

DEE-JAY Thank you very much sir. Now I wonder if you would mind telling the listeners how you . . .

PATIENT Correction! I wasn't thinking. If they drained their blood in advance then there'll be no blood spattering around when the bullets land would there?

DEE-JAY I imagine not sir.

PATIENT So there you are. What's an execution without letting blood eh? Hm. I suppose they could always hang them. No. That's no use either. There's got to be blood. It's shooting. Nothing else would do.

DEE-JAY Well, thank you sir. I hope you enjoy the show.

PATIENT Wait a minute. Am I still on the air?

DEE-JAY Certainly sir.

PATIENT In that case . . . *(He clears his throat, sings:)*

Blood, blood, glorious blood
Nothing quite like it for offering to God
Banish the gallows
So I can wallow
In the crimson juice of the criminal sod!

Blood, blood, copious blood
I'd happily drown if this earth it would flood

[78]

It's blood I feel well on
So puncture the felon
Give glory to God and make gory your god.

(He breaks into a fit of coughing, followed by spasms and expires.)

NURSE *(feels for his pulse, finding none, closes his eyes and picks up his feet)* I think he died happy. *(Drags him out by the feet.)*

DEE-JAY Oh dear. A-ah. . . here comes a familiar face. A neighbour of mine to be precise. *(Enter a Woman, angry-looking, herding five children.)* Neighbour! You look angry. What's the matter?

NEIGHBOUR What's the matter? I've divorced that foolish man that's all. Packed out of his house. He had the nerve to say we would stay at home and watch the shooting on television. The children said they wanted to see it live and I agreed with them. Television is not the same thing. We spent so much time arguing I'm sure we have missed all the best seats. God punish him! *(Exit, with brood.)*

DEE-JAY *(using his binoculars)* The moment approaches. Macheath is on the way. From this distance I can say that he looks calm, unruffled, ready to meet his Maker. He has gambled his last, bedded his last and butchered his last. When the moment comes, there shall pass over this city a great gust of wind. That sound which you may or may not hear at home, those of you who are watching the scene on your television, will be the sigh of relief from the entire populace. And here comes . . . if my eyes do not deceive me . . .

(Enter Chief Anikura and De Madam. Brown follows, sneaks in and hides in a corner.)

DEE-JAY Chief Anikura, would you like to say a word to . . . *(Chief Anikura makes a rude noise. Dee-Jay recoils.)*

DE MADAM Good for him, the cheeky sod!

DEE-JAY I think what the Chief was trying to say is, No Comment.

(Enter Polly and the Syndicate. They stand on the opposite side. Polly is uncomfortable, undecided. Suddenly she breaks into a run to their side, sobbing.)

DE MADAM *(comforting her)* There there, dearie. Blood will out. I always said it, blood's thicker than water. *(Polly bursts into louder sobbing.)*

[79]

ANIKURA   Now you've gone and done it Cecilia.

DE MADAM   What did I do?

ANIKURA   Don't mention blood to her!

DE MADAM   Oh dear, and she such a sensitive child. Got that from me you know. Maybe you'd better not watch, Polly. What do you think? Shall I take you home?

POLLY   *(recovers suddenly)* Oh no, I'll be all right. I ought to stand by him to the last. It wouldn't be right for me to miss it would it?

ANIKURA   Quite right. Loyalty. That, she got from me.

(Strains of 'Just a closer walk with thee', increasing in volume. Enter the Bevy of Whores, led by Sukie, doing a single-line dance to the tune.)

DEE-JAY   Do my eyes deceive me? There's your answer. For those bleeding-heart *cynics* and *liberals* who say that Public Execution is bad for public morale, behold the perfect answer. The entire female habituees of Playboy Club, the famous whorehouse of Madame Gbafe have been converted. To the last tit they have joined the CSU and here they come singing a different tune from that which we used to hear. Oh the age of miracles! Nothing like a public execution to melt the hardiest heart of stone. It's a sight to touch the most depraved heart. *(Wipes a tear.)* I am saved! I too am saved! Wash me clean in the blood of Mackie sorry — I mean in the blood of the Lord, Amen! I am saved sister, come round the corner and I'll show you.

(He dashes to the front, partners Sukie and dances out. He later re-appears in his booth with his arms round Sukie, during Mackie's farewell song. Enter Macheath, in a contraption not unlike a tumbril. He is wheeled to the execution spot. Prophet Jeru, a Roman Catholic priest, an Anglican, an Imam, and a Sango priest detach themselves from the crowd and move towards Macheath.)

CATHOLIC   He's mine. He's taken Mass with us.

ANGLICAN   He's mine. I baptized him.

JERU   He's mine. I officiated at his wedding.

IMAN   He's mine. We celebrated Ileya[22] together.

SANGO PRIEST   Lightning is about to strike him. He's mine. Plus his property.[23]

OFFICER   Which of them do you acknowledge, prisoner?

MACHEATH   *(points to the Sango priest)* I like his style. *(The others protest.)* After all, property is what it's all about, not so?

[80]

(The Sango priest grins.) Also, as it happens, I have none left. Nothing. *(All the priests retire, disgusted.)* Vultures!

POLLY *(moving towards him)* Oh Mackie you defiant soul, I knew you'd remain the same whatever happens.

MACK Don't talk such nonsense. Have you ever seen anyone remain the same after he's been pierced by several bullets?

OFFICER Have you any last pronouncements to make sir before we perform our side of the business?

MACK Thank you officer. Your subtlety, your finesse is most impressive.

OFFICER *(looking at his watch)* Make it brief.

MACK I shall be brief. Tell your men to take positions and take aim. When I have finished I shall raise my lace hand-kerchief like this and say 'So long'. They are to fire immediately. Speed and accuracy shall be greatly appreciated.

OFFICER The Army will oblige. *(He returns to squad.)* Positions! Aim! Hold your fire until I signal. Proceed Mr Macheath.

Mackie's Farewell

> I hate to see the morning sun come up
> I hate to see the morning sun come up
> For it reminds me that my hour is up
> Feeling tomorrow is not a thing I'll know
> Feeling tomorrow is not a thing I'll know
> Instead I'll be filling a hole down below

> I'd like to tell you that I forgive you all
> Who have done things to bring about my fall
> You rotten policemen who double-crossed Mackie
> At least I know I'm not the Emperor's lackey
> You venal women who betrayed your man
> That's the way you've been since the world began
> So if I tell you that I forgive you all
> That's the same as saying, I hope you roast in he-e-ell!

Chorus:

> I've got the imperial blues
> I'm as blue as I can be
> But not as blue as I'll be
> In the face as the bullets hit me
> Or grey or blue-black or whatever niggers are when they

[81]

quench
I love my Emperor
I'm crazy 'bout the little terror
I think he's crazy too
He really belongs in the zoo

MACKIE   And who knows when he'll send you to join me in the cold, cold trench.

CHORUS   And who knows when he'll send us to join you in the cold cold trench.

MACKIE   So please forgive me if I have done you wrong
And mind you kiss the Emperor's arse if your life you would prolong
Mackie is going now who's been with you . . . so long.
(As the song reaches the very end and Mackie's hand raised half-way up, a siren is heard fast approaching.)

DEE-JAY   What's this? The Emperor's Extraordinary Courier!

CROWD   The Emperor! Long live the Emperor! Long live the Emperor! Vive Vive Vive l'Empereur! Vive Vive Vive l'Empereur! Vive Vive Vive l'Empereur!
(Preceded by a trumpeter blowing a fanfare, the Courier races towards the Dee-Jay with a scroll.

COURIER   *(lifts his hand. Silence.)* Read the proclamation.

DEE-JAY   'We, Our Serene Highness, newly reincarnated, and crowned Emperor Charlemagne Desiree Boky the First, Lion of Bangui, Tiger of the Tropics, Elect of God, First among Kings and Emperors, the Pulsing Nugget of Life, and Radiating Sun of Africa hereby pronounce, in honour of our coronation on this day, a general Amnesty for all common criminals. Take heed however, that this great condescension shall not, repeat shall not extend to anyone accused or convicted of crimes of a political nature. Long live the Emperor!'

COURIER   Long live the Emperor!

CROWD   Long live the Emperor! Long live the Imperial Family! Mackie's saved. He's saved. Saved! Three hearty cheers for the Emperor. Hip Hip Hip Hurray! Hip Hip Hip Hurray! Hip Hip Hip Hurray!

ANIKURA   *(steps forward and addresses audience)* Well, does that surprise you? It shouldn't. We men of influence — of power if you like — respect one another. We speak the same language, so we usually work things out. As for you lot,

[82]

Remember, it's not everyday
The Emperor's Courier timely arrives
Repairing wrongs, sustaining rights
And neatly installing the Back-to-Square-One.
And watch out! Beware certain well-tuned voices
That clamour loudest: 'Justice-for-all'!
A ragged coat does not virtue make
— Here I stand as your prime example —
Nor is the predator a champion of rights,
A brave Robin Hood equalizing the loot
It's too easy to declare society fair game —
For proof, my son-in-law is more than ample.
What we must look for is the real beneficiary
Who does it profit? That question soon
Overtakes all your slogans — who gains?
Who really accumulates and exercises
Power over others. The currency of that power
Though it forms the bone of contention
Soon proves secondary. I tell you —
Power is delicious *(turns sharply)* Heel!

*(Immediately the Beggars shuffle towards him. Mackie
next snaps his fingers. Polly, followed by the gang, gather
round him. The band strikes up the tune of* Mack the
Knife.
*Enter Boky in his Imperial robes, drawn in a chariot by four
stalwarts. He drives across, and a procession forms behind
him in the following order: The Priests; the Uniformed
Services; Chief Anikura and Macheath who first go
through a dumb-play of 'After-you' courtesies; then fall in
step with each other, followed by their women; the Gangs;
the Whores; the General Rabble.)*

The End.

[83]

Appendix

DEE-JAY　We've taken over. It's as simple as that. In case it has escaped your notice, I'm laying it on you man, we've taken over. I mean, man, get wise, when did you last see a *live* band back home, I mean live man? A *real live* band with living musicians? Okay Okay, so when some society fatso wants to spray, he gets a band together someplace and gets some sweaty foreheads to stick Murtalas[1] on. But that's special man, that's *occasion.* We're talking about real life, dig? So I'll just introduce myself. I'm your M.C.D.J. — Master of Ceremonies Disc-Jockey. Or Master of Ceremonies or Disc Jockey. Or simply Dee-jay. Take your Choice. See what I mean? You got a choice. You don't get a choice with a live band. And you don't get much choice between live-band or Dee-jays, cause the home country is broke see? And when that country goes broke you know what goes first. If you don't, ask the Universities. Well, Dee-jays come cheap, that's why I'm hosting this show. One time we called it the Way-Out Opera — for short, Opera Wayo. Call it the Beggars' Opera if you insist — that's what the whole nation is doing — begging for a slice of the action.

And don't think it's the kind of begging you're used to. Here the beggars say 'Give me a slice of the action or — *(demonstrating)* — give me a slice off your throat. Man, some beggars! You know what, why don't you just make up your own title as we go along because, I tell you brother, I'm yet to decide whether such a way-out opera should be named after the beggars, the Army, the bandits, the Police, the Cash-madams, the Students, the trade-unionists, the Alhajis and Alhajas, the Aladura, the Academicas, the Holy Patriarchs and Unholy Heresiarchs — I mean man, in this way-out country everyone acts way out. Including the traffic. Maybe we should call it, the Trafficking Opera. Which just complicates things with

[84]

trafficking in foreign exchange. Nice topical touch. Man, this country whips you right out on cloud Nine! I'd better bring you back to earth with a song about that universal species of humanity—and if you haven't heard Louis Armstrong do his own thing with good old Mack, man, just where you been? One a-Two-a-Three—take it from there Baby. Let's go.

Textual Notes

[1] MURTALAS: Local slang for 20 Naira notes

[2] IGBETI: A village in Western Nigeria whose rich marble resources have become the monopoly of a private group. Several mysterious deaths have overtaken the champions of public rights to the marble. (This deposit has since been taken over by the Civilian government in Oyo State: 1979)

[3] OGAH SAH: Big Chief Sir.
OGA SA: Big Chief turn tail.

[4] RANKA DEDE: A very respectful salutation of feudal origin.

[5] IKOYI: A Lagos elite suburbia.

[6] TAPHY: A by-word now for the authorized flogging of Nigerian citizens by soldiers for alleged traffic infractions etc. Neither women nor the elderly were spared this experience of public humiliation.

[7] SUZIES: Local for dashing young women.

[8] UDOJI: Named for the 1975 wages review commission which created Nigeria's record inflation.

[9] OTI O: Never Never!

[10] BAR BEACH SHOW: The Bar Beach became the public execution arena in Lagos for Nigeria's armed robbers.

[11] AWOOF: Booty.

[12] A reference to General Gowon's wedding during the Nigerian Civil War. Commemoratory stamps were printed and launched throughout Nigerian embassies while this then Head of State claimed the (late) capture of a Biafran stronghold as his wedding present.

[13] An actual incident. Fed up with the public obscenity of corpses in public places, Tai Solarin, a tireless reformer and former Public Complaints Commissioner obtained a plain coffin and, with some helpers, personally scooped the decomposed remains of a 35-day old corpse on a public highway into the coffin and presented it to the Lagos City Council.

[14] ATTACK TRADE: Named for the brisk across-the-lines business during the Civil War.

[15] FARANSE: The French, or black francophones.

[16] BEEN-TOS: Been to Europe and 'abroad'.

[17] GARI: A West African staple food. A farina.

[18] SHARIA: The Moslem religious law. There was then strong agitation for its elevation to the Federal Appeal level in Nigeria. (The Iranian example may yet resurrect such piety.)

[19] IDOBALE NI MO WA: Respectfully prostrated am I.

[20] SECRET SOCIETIES: The quotes are from a government directive on the subject, a typical overkill response to the sudden wave of sanctimonious denunciations by the Nigerian public. There are of course *evil* secret societies.

[21] Actual suggestions in Readers' Letters to newspapers.

[22] ILEYA: Moslem Festival.

[23] SANGO: God of Thunder and Lightning. Kills his victims, and his priests claim their property.